How to Settle Your Own Personal Injury Case

How to Settle Your Own Personal Injury Case

Winning Big Without Hiring a Lawyer

Martin Zevin

A Citadel Press Book

Published by Carol Publishing Group

A Citadel Press Book
Published by Carol Publishing Group
Citadel Press is a registered trademark of Carol Communications, Inc.
Editorial Offices: 600 Madison Avenue, New York, N.Y. 10022
Sales & Distribution Offices: 120 Enterprise Avenue, Secaucus, N.J. 07094
In Canada: Canadian Manda Group, One Atlantic Avenue, Suite 105, Toronto, Ontario M6K 3E7
Queries regarding rights and permissions should be addressed to Carol Publishing Group, 600 Madison Avenue, New York, N.Y. 10022

Carol Publishing Group books are available at special discounts for bulk purchases, sales promotions, fund-raising, or educational purposes. Special editions can be created to specifications. For details, contact: Special Sales Department, Carol Publishing Group, 120 Enterprise Avenue, Secaucus, N.J. 07094

Manufactured in the United States of America

10 9 8 7 6 5 4 3 2 1

Library of Congress Cataloging-in-Publication Data

Zevin, Martin.
How to settle your own personal injury case : winning big without hiring a lawyer / Martin Zevin.
p. cm.
"A Citadel Press book."
ISBN 0–8065–1684–4
1. Personal injuries—United States—Popular works. 2. Trial practice—United States—Popular works. 3. Pro se representation--United States—Popular works. I. Title.
KF1257.Z9Z48 1995
346.7303'23—dc20
[347.306323] 95–9375
CIP

To Dotty, my beautiful wife of twenty years, and David, our wonderful son. You are the loving lights of my life.

Contents

Charts, Checklists, and Sample Letters

Author to Reader

I have been a personal injury lawyer in Florida for over twenty years. There are three lawyers in my firm, five secretaries, and a part-time bookkeeper. We've been averaging about one million dollars a year in gross income, mostly from personal injury cases. My own income is usually $200,000 a year. That puts me above the average but certainly nowhere near the top of the list of thousands of lawyers in the United States who specialize in winning money for injured clients.

All of those lawyers are going to be very unhappy that I've written this book, and unhappier still if the book is a big success. They will say that an injured person must have a lawyer to properly protect his legal rights. Read this book, and decide for yourself.

Most personal injury cases are settled without a lawsuit. This is duc to the nature of the system, and it is true throughout the United States. Depending on the state, lawyers will charge between 25 percent to 50 percent of the total recovery. The average is about 33⅓ percent if settled without a lawsuit, or 40 percent if a lawsuit is filed. There is usually an additional fee of 5 percent or 10 percent if there is an appeal.

As an example, let's say you have been rear-ended while driving your car. Your neck and back are injured. An MRI scan shows you have bulging discs in your neck and back, but no herniations. Many factors will be discussed to determine the value of your case, but let's say it's worth $30,000. A lawyer takes your case and settles it fairly quickly without a lawsuit. He may take 1/3, or $10,000, off the top as his fee. You may have $4,000 in outstanding medical bills that have to come out of the remaining $20,000. The lawyer also charges you $2,000 for his costs, which may include medical reports and private investigator's bills. Moreover, some lawyers charge for their office overhead expenses, like photocopies, postage, and telephone calls. So, out of a $30,000 settlement, you end up with $14,000. (See Chart A, page xiv)

If you follow the advice in this book, you may be able to settle the case on your own. Maybe the insurance adjuster will only offer you a maximum of $25,000 because you don't have a lawyer. You will still have to pay the outstanding medical bills, although the doctors may reduce their balances from $4,000 to $2,500 because you're paying "out of your pocket," especially if they've already been paid some money by an insurance company. You could save $1,500 in unnecessary costs, because you won't need an investigator, the doctors won't charge you as much for their reports as they charge the lawyer, and you won't be running up big office overhead tabs. So, even if you settle on your own for $25,000 instead of $30,000, you would end up with $22,000 in your pocket instead of the $14,000 with a lawyer. (See Chart B, page xiv)

Yes, I, or some other personal injury lawyer, will have lost an easy $10,000 fee. But we'll get over it. We'll just have to work harder on the more difficult cases, the ones that really require a lawyer. (See chapter 16)

Why hasn't a book like this been written before? It should be obvious. No lawyer has ever wanted to kill the goose that lays the golden egg.

If you learn only one thing from this book, let it be this: The more knowledge you have, the more money you will put in your pocket. The way to get the knowledge is to take advantage of free consultations with personal injury lawyers. You will learn what questions to ask about your case, your state's laws, your insurance policy, and the doctors you should see.

In this book you will receive the tools and strategies for successful negotiating. You still need to have the knowledge from your free consultations to properly use these tactics. You can't negotiate effectively with an adjuster until you know how much your case is worth. You won't know the value of your case without the legal consultations. Likewise, if you decide you need a lawyer, you can't negotiate properly with him until you know the value of your case and what other lawyers are charging.

Knowledge is the key. I hope this book opens some doors that were locked to you. Unlocking the remaining doors is up to you. By reading this book, you are well on your way to successfully negotiating, if you are ever injured.

Remember though, that the scope of this book has been limited to personal injury claims. Of course, you may be able to get free consultations with lawyers that may be useful in many other areas, such as divorce, real estate, probate, and bankruptcy. Those free consultations will give you a greater understanding and knowledge of your rights, of whether or not you need a lawyer, and how much a reasonable fee would be.

You can also use these basic negotiating techniques in all aspects of your life. Life is about being both a giver and a receiver. If you can balance the two, you've got it made.

July 1995
Boca Raton, Florida

CHART A

Sample Settlement—$30,000 with lawyer

Gross:	$30,000
Less $33^{1}/_{3}$% Attorney's fee:	− 10,000
	$20,000
Less Legal costs:	
A. Medical report fees	− 1,000
B. Private investigators	− 600
C. Copying charges, postage, telephone and miscellaneous office expenses	− 400
	$18,000
Less medical bills:	− 4,000
Net to you:	$14,000

CHART B

Sample settlement—$25,000 without lawyer

Gross:	$25,000
Less costs (medical reports only—reduced by doctor from $1,000):	− 500
	$24,500
Less medical bills ($4,000 reduced by doctors to $2,500):	− 2,500
Net to you:	$22,000

How to Settle Your Own Personal Injury Case

CHAPTER 1

What to Do If You're Injured

I hope you never need the information in this book. If you live your whole life without getting injured, you are lucky and blessed. But most of us will have one or more injuries during our lives. Many of these accidents will be our own fault. Many of your injuries will heal up quickly and be forgotten. If you just have a temporary injury or the accident is your fault, this book won't help you.

Also, the scope of this book is limited to personal injury claims. I won't be discussing any other legal matters such as divorce, bankruptcy, probate, contracts, real estate, etc. However, you should be able to use some of the basic ideas in this book to help you in all parts of your life, including legal areas.

Let's get back to the example in the introduction—you have been rear-ended while driving your car. You are stopped at a red light, minding your own business, when somebody plows right into you, hard. You're wearing your shoulder belt, but your body still shoots forward and back, and your head strikes against the headrest. Your left knee jams into the dashboard. Your fingers are compressed tightly against the wheel at the moment of impact.

You are in shock. You are a thirty-seven-year-old married woman. You're a 4th grade teacher. You were on your way home from school. The bus will be dropping off your two kids soon, and your husband will be back from work around six expecting supper. You don't know what to do. You feel dazed and lightheaded. Your left knee hurts, and your fingers are tingling. Suddenly, you're aware of honking. Somebody is knocking on your window. You're not sure if you blacked out for a second, and you're angry, confused, afraid.

The knocking on your window continues. You roll it down. It's a man in a suit. "Are you okay, miss? I'm really sorry. I was just looking in my glove compartment for a tape and bang! Are you okay?"

What do you do? You feel as though you should get out and see how bad the damage is to your car, but you are still feeling dizzy.

Though you are not thinking about it, your case has just begun. Everything that happens from this moment on will be important in determining the amount of your settlement. Don't get out of the car. Ask the man who hit you to call the police and an ambulance. It's important for your health that you get medical treatment in the nearest emergency room, just to be sure there are no broken bones or other problems that could get much worse without immediate care (particularly, back and neck injuries). It is also important for your case that your initial physical complaints are listed in the hospital records. Naturally, the accident report prepared by the police officer is also very important to verify who hit you, what insurance he has, witnesses, etc. Try to get the case number and/or the investigating officer's name.

Everything we are discussing now presumes you are truly hurt. Certain problems, particularly sprains and strains in the neck and back, may not be immediately noticeable, or may not feel as uncomfortable right after the accident as they do sometime later. But you must be legitimately hurt to make a claim for personal injury. Insurance fraud is a criminal offense. Faking injuries to get a settlement is stealing.

Even if you get away with it, it will come back to haunt you. Chances are that someday you'll be seriously injured, and that old fake claim that you settled for very little will work against you. Insurance companies and defense attorneys always look for pre-existing injuries to try to prove that you already had a problem before your new accident. So use what you learn here when you really need it. If you are not hurt, be sure you still make the accident report, settle up your car damage, and be thankful that you're okay. If you start hurting later on, immediately consult a doctor.

Let's get back to our case. You are taken by ambulance to the emergency room while the police officer fills out the report, and your car is towed away. By the time the doctor sees you, you have a bad headache and your neck and back are getting stiff. Some of the fingers in your left hand feel numb, and the right hand is still tingling. Your left knee is swollen and pounding. Be sure to report all of your problems in the emergency room. Repeat them to anyone who questions you: paramedics, nurses, doctors. The ambulance attendant who first saw you will be preparing his own report, so let him know everything in detail, too.

Right now, your knee and head are hurting you the most, but in a month, your back may be killing you. If your whole body is aching now, let everybody know it. Remember, all of these records will be closely examined six months or a year from now, when you are trying to settle your case. Don't lie about anything, but don't overlook anything either.

At the emergency room they take X rays of your neck, back, head, left knee, and both hands. They tell you that nothing is broken. They give you two prescriptions; one is a muscle relaxant and the other a pain killer. They discharge you with some instruction sheets and the name of a doctor to see if you are still hurting in the morning. You call your husband to pick you up. You won't be cooking dinner tonight.

What about the bills? You can expect to get them from the ambulance company, hospital, radiology department, emergency room doctor, and maybe even the lab, if they took some blood, plus the cost of those prescriptions. Who is supposed to pay? At the hospital, they asked you for your hospital and medical insurance cards. You have group insurance through the school board, but there's a $500 deductible you haven't satisfied, and after that they only pay 80 percent. They also asked you for your car insurance card. But why? The accident wasn't your fault.

Many states have no-fault laws for car accidents. In these states, everyone who owns a car must have insurance to pay for their own medical bills from a car accident, even if it's the other person's fault. This is sometimes called Personal Injury Protection, or P.I.P. In some states, it's optional. Other states have no P.I.P., but they do have medical payments coverage. This pays anywhere from 20 percent to 100 percent of your bills, up to a certain limit. If you have anything like this, your car insurance is considered "primary," which means that it pays before any other insurance, including private or group coverage, Blue Cross/Blue Shield, Medicare, etc. These other companies may pay some or all of the balance. If you get a settlement down the road, some of these secondary insurance companies may have a subrogation lien, which means they are entitled to get some of their money back. You will have to negotiate with them just as you will be negotiating with the insurance company of the man who hit you.

Right now, all you want to do is get home and fall into bed. What's taking that husband of yours so long anyway?

Checklist I (Immediately Following the Accident)

1. Stay in the car.
2. Ask the other driver to call the police and ambulance.
3. Tell paramedics everything that's hurting you.
4. Ask the police officer for all information about the other driver, insurance coverage, and witnesses.
5. Go to the emergency room by ambulance. Give a detailed account of all your injuries.
6. Give the hospital billing staff information on your car insurance and any group or private health insurance.

CHAPTER 2

The Day After

You wake up so sore you can hardly move. You are barely able to reach over to the phone. You call in sick. Before you flop back into bed, you need to make at least one more call. Report the accident to your insurance company, and get a claim number. If you don't know the number of your claim department, get it from your agent. Be sure to explain not only the details of the accident, but also the full extent of your injuries. Tell them about the ambulance and the hospital, and that you plan to see a doctor. Also tell them you had to miss work.

If your insurance includes Personal Injury Protection (P.I.P.), you will normally be able to recover at least 60 percent of your lost wages, tax free. (Incidentally, the settlement you are going to receive is also tax free—at least from federal taxes.) You can generally get the money for lost wages even if you are still paid at work, as long as you have to use up sick leave or vacation time.

P.I.P. coverage also will pay for most of your medical bills. Generally, the adjuster will pay out medical bills and lost wages as they come in. And if it appears that your injury will keep you out of work for a long time, request, in writing, that all P.I.P. benefits be reserved for paying your lost wages. Most insurance companies will honor this request.

Remember, you want to take full advantage of all the benefits your insurance provides. This is why you have been paying the premiums for all those years. You are a safe driver who has never made a claim. Your premiums should not be raised, because the accident was not your fault. However, in most states, there is no guarantee that making a claim won't affect your premium. Even so, you'd be foolish not to make the claim and lose out on many thousands of dollars in benefits. For the next six months, your medical bills alone could run anywhere from a few thousand, to ten or even twenty thousand dollars. In addition, you could have hundreds or thousands of dollars in lost wages.

Before you read farther, check out your car insurance coverage right now. Call your agent. Be sure you have the maximum available coverage (with no deductible) for medical bills and lost wages. This is important, even if you have your own private or group medical insurance and disability income insurance. Remember, if you have to go through your private or group medical coverage, you may have to pay some, or all, of that money back from your settlement, and you may have to pay the deductible out of your pocket. You can still, however, collect from P.I.P. for lost income and also from your separate disability insurance (after all, you are paying two separate premiums).

There is another extremely important coverage you must have to protect yourself—uninsured and underinsured motorist, usually abbreviated U.M. Some states do not require car owners to have any personal injury liability coverage. In other states, there may be a requirement for a minimum amount of personal injury liability coverage. What does this mean? Let's get back to our sample case to find out.

You are lying in bed, hurting all over. You've just hung up, having reported your accident. Ask your husband to get out your car insurance policy. Okay, there it is: you have $50,000 per person, and $100,000 per occurrence in uninsured motorist coverage. You have the same coverage for both your car and your husband's. Once you get a copy of the accident report (usually available from the police department within a few days), you'll see the name and policy number of the insurance company of the guy who hit you. In some states, you may already have a driver exchange form which gives you this information.

Call up directory assistance for 800 numbers, and you should be able to get that company's claim department. Phone and find out if the other driver has reported the accident yet. If he has, the adjuster may be willing to give you the amount of his personal injury liability coverage over the phone; otherwise, he will give you an address to use to request the information in writing.

You can also set up an appointment for an appraiser to estimate your property damage. If you deal directly with the other company, you'll avoid having to pay out the deductible from your collision coverage. If you collect from your own company, it will then take awhile until the other driver's company pays back your company. Eventually, you will get a reimbursement for your deductible. The only advantage to settling the property damage under your own collision coverage is that the claim will usually be processed faster, especially if you have a reliable company. Also, if you have substantial damage to your car, be sure you take lots of pictures before any repair work is done. These pictures will be important six months or a year from now, when you're negotiating to settle your personal injury case.

Let's get back to the personal injury part of the claim. You find out that the other driver has personal injury liability coverage of $50,000 per person, $100,000 per occurrence. What does this mean? What is the most you can collect in your case, assuming you have a serious enough injury? Let's refer to Chart C below.

Chart C

I. Other Driver's personal injury liability coverage:
$ 50,000 per person
$100,000 per occurrence

II. Uninsured Motorist Coverage on your car:
$ 50,000 per person
$100,000 per occurrence

III. Uninsured Motorist Coverage on your husband's car:
$ 50,000 per person
$100,000 per occurrence

The maximum amount you can get (from the insurance coverage shown) may be $50,000, $100,000, or $150,000 depending on the laws of each state. Stacking is permitted in some states. Stacking means that you can add up the uninsured motorist coverage on each vehicle in your household for which you pay a premium. So, if your state allows stacking, you would actually have coverage of $100,000 per person, $200,000 per occurrence. Since you were the only one injured in the accident, forget about the "per occurrence" coverage. This might apply if your husband and children were also in the car. Then, the highest coverage you could have together would be $200,000, but no more than $100,000 to any one person.

Also, in some states, the law allows you to use your uninsured motorist coverage regardless of how much coverage the other driver has. As a practical matter, though, if the other driver has enough insurance to cover your injuries, your company will not pay you anything from the uninsured motorist coverage.

But let's say your injury turns out to be very serious. The other driver's insurance company may offer you the full $50,000 policy limit, and you may then try to get up to $100,000 from your own company. But watch out; don't accept any policy limit amount from another company and sign a release when you are still trying to get more money from your company. More about this later.

Some states may not allow stacking, or you may have, unknowingly, waived stacking from your policy. In that case, you would only have $50,000 U.M. per person. The law in some states may say that your uninsured motorist coverage must be larger than the other driver's liability insurance, and you can only collect the difference from your company. For example, if the other driver had $100,000 liability, and you had $250,000 U.M., you could only get his $100,000, and then no more than another $150,000 from your own U.M.

In such a state, with our sample case, where you may have nonstacking $50,000 U.M. and the other driver had $50,000 liability, you would be limited to his $50,000 and you could not get any more from your company. That's why I said that you could collect a maximum of $50,000, $100,000, or $150,000 depending on the laws of your state. It gets even more complicated if you are injured while a passenger in someone else's car. Then their uninsured motorist coverage comes into the picture. And if the driver who caused the accident was driving a rented car, or someone else's car, then it can really become crazy.

Are you confused? Well, that is why personal injury lawyers are around. A good personal injury lawyer will look at every possible source of insurance coverage to try to maximize the potential recovery. The main thing you need to know, when you make that call to your agent to check on your coverage, is to get the maximum possible uninsured motorist coverage, and to take stacking, if it's available.

Okay, you have made the call to your insurance company to report the claim. You have called your agent to check on your coverage, and you have added and increased the coverages as I've suggested. You're not quite ready to take a nap yet. As long as you are laid up in bed anyway, get comfortable with the phone and the Yellow Pages. You are about to get smart fast.

Checklist II (Day After the Accident)

1. Call work. Be sure your time lost due to the injury is recorded.
2. Report the accident to your car insurance company. Get a claim number.
3. Review your car insurance coverage with your agent. Make the necessary changes.
4. Contact the other driver's insurance company. Set up a property damage appraisal. Ask for the limits of personal injury liability.
5. Have pictures taken of the property damage.

CHAPTER 3

Calling Lawyers for Free Advice, or, Eating the Fruit of Knowledge

Turn the Yellow Pages to the listings for "Attorneys." You'll probably see anywhere from a few pages of ads, to over a hundred pages. Would you believe that, until 1977, lawyers were prohibited from any kind of advertising? Then, suddenly, the U.S. Supreme Court said it was okay. Now you can't go through the day without getting bombarded by lawyers advertising on television, billboards, bus benches, newpapers, radio, mail and, of course, in the friendly Yellow Pages.

When advertising first became legal, I was a struggling young lawyer trying to make it on my own. I was one of the first lawyers in Florida to advertise in newspapers, which was the only legal form allowed at that time. All the other lawyers hated me, but I figured I didn't have much to lose, except the relatively small cost of a few ads.

At the time, I had a general practice, so I figured I would advertise simple legal services at fees much lower than the norm, to try to attract new business. I advertised a fee of $300 for uncontested divorces when most lawyers were charging $500 to $5,000. (Now you may see them advertised for $100 or less.) I advertised simple wills for $25 when most lawyers were charging $100 to $500. Suddenly, the phone was ringing off the hook. The reason I mention this is that although the scope of this book is limited to personal injury cases, many of the negotiating tactics you will learn here can help you get attorneys to reduce their fees in all types of cases.

The lawyers who were overcharging hated me, but the public loved me. Newspapers did articles on me, printing copies of my ad on their front pages. For a while, I was famous, at least in my area. More importantly it allowed me to become established and to eventually concentrate on personal injury cases. I changed my ads and began advertising my contingent fees at 30 percent without suit. The usual was 33⅓ percent to 40 percent, whether the lawyer filed suit or not. If suit was filed, I advertised at 35 percent, still considerably lower than most of my competition. Again, business blossomed and flourished.

Then, television advertising was allowed, and I chose not to become an instant television celebrity. Several of my fellow lawyers did make big names for themselves on TV, and their practices boomed. But I felt content with my relative success, and I began concentrating more on referrals from previous clients, doctors, and other lawyers. I still advertise in the Yellow Pages (as do most personal injury lawyers these days) and in some local papers.

Why have I digressed about advertising? The U.S. Supreme Court decided it was okay because it is a first amendment right: the right to free speech. But they also decided it was okay because they felt it was more likely to help people rather than hurt them. And, for the most part, advertising has helped. It has brought down the cost of many routine services. It has also slightly lowered the contingency fees of some lawyers in personal injury cases. It has made the public less afraid of lawyers and more likely to call for free consultations regarding their rights. Now it's time for you to really take advantage of this situation.

You are about to eat of the fruit of knowledge. It's waiting there before you, in the Yellow Pages under "Attorneys." Read the ads. They all beckon. "Talk to a Lawyer. It's Free." "Don't get hurt twice—know your legal rights." "Injured? On call 24 hours." "All of your questions answered, including how much is your case worth?"

Personal injury lawyers are all fighting each other to try to get your case. Each one offers free consultation, by phone or in person, to try to persuade you that he or she is the right one for you. They are willing to give you the apple of knowledge, but you still have the freedom of choice. You may choose to speak to another lawyer and get his advice, and then a third, and a fourth. And you don't have to hire any of them. It's like shopping for a home. You can have a realtor show you many listed homes without buying one. The more you see, the more you'll know about the value of a deal, whether it's listed or whether you buy it directly from an owner. It's your knowledge of the market that gives you the big edge.

Each time you speak to another lawyer, you'll be gaining valuable knowledge about your case, knowledge that ultimately may allow you to settle the case without a lawyer. Incidentally, feel free to follow recommendations by family or friends, as long as the lawyers they recommend specialize in personal injury cases. If you already have a lawyer who has handled other matters for you, ask him to recommend a personal injury specialist. However, be aware that your lawyer will probably want a referral fee from the specialist, which is likely to increase the proposed contingency fee. I'm recommending the Yellow Pages since it contains so many ads. Use it and you're bound to speak to at least three or four lawyers, if you make enough calls.

Your experiences now will also help you get some clues as to which lawyers you may wish to consider down the road, if you decide that the offer you get on your own is not enough. So get out a pad, and start taking notes on each call you make. You may end up referring to these notes six months, or a year from now.

One thing you'll notice immediately is the response time to your call. Let's say you make ten calls in one day. You tell the receptionist you were just in a car accident yesterday, and you need to speak to a lawyer as soon as possible. Perhaps one or two of your ten calls will result in your speaking to a lawyer immediately. The other eight or nine times, you'll be leaving a message. By the end of the day, you may get return calls from three or four other lawyers. Two or three other lawyers may call you the following day. You may not hear from the others for several days, or maybe not at all.

You should cross off this last group from your list for the future—they have already proven themselves unreliable. The ones you speak to immediately, or who return your call fairly promptly, should already be scoring some points in their favor.

One of the biggest complaints by clients about their lawyers is "He never returns my calls," or "I never know what's going on." If a lawyer doesn't respond quickly to your initial call, chances are he's going to be even worse when he has you as a client. Of course, lawyers are often busy in court, or out of the office taking depositions, but they should still be diligent enough to call for their messages during their free time.

Okay, now you're speaking to a lawyer. He'll be asking a lot of the questions first, so he can size up your case. Remember, he's looking to pick a credible client with a good case, just as you are trying to get some information from a good lawyer. Be yourself. Be totally honest and sincere. Answer all his questions. Then ask a lot of your own. Ask him what the law is in your state regarding the use of uninsured motorist coverage and stacking. You should have handy all the information about your policy and your husband's, as well as the coverage of the driver who hit you.

Discuss not only the coverages, but also the specific insurance companies. Ask the lawyer to rate the other driver's insurance company and your own. The same case can have a widely different value depending on which insurance companies are involved. Then ask him for recommendations of those car insurance companies that offer the highest settlements and that pay promptly. This will be valuable information for you to consider in the future. If several lawyers tell you that your insurance company is consistently low in evaluating claims, change to a better company. It is much more important to be insured by a generous company, than to be paying the lowest available premium. In fact, some of the biggest and best known companies may charge relatively high premiums and yet offer low estimates for claims. Remember, insurance companies earn greater profits if they charge more and pay out less.

Also, ask the lawyer what is the statute of limitations in your state, because if you don't settle your case or file a lawsuit before the period expires, your claim is dead. Most states will require that the claim be settled, or suit filed within 2–4 years. If your state has a short statute of limitations, the course of action you take may be very different than if you had more time.

Naturally, you should ask him about his normal contingency fee, and how it's figured. Remember, he will be telling you his normal fee—many lawyers will be willing to take a lower fee to get your good case. Ask him if he requires that you pay for costs up front, such as doctor's reports, private investigators, and court costs if a lawsuit is filed. Also, does he charge you for office overhead costs, like copies, postage, and long distance calls. Look for a firm that never asks for money up front and that waives office costs as part of doing business. Many firms charge substantial amounts for costs, which can seriously reduce your net recovery.

Ask him how much your case is worth. Many lawyers advertise that they will answer this question in their free consultation. He may try to set up an appointment to see you. If you like him enough on the phone, it can't hurt to meet him personally. If you plan to try to settle the case yourself, you won't hire him now, but you'll know him personally if you need him later.

Since you were just injured yesterday, it will be difficult for any lawyer to pinpoint an exact value of your case. More likely, a good lawyer can give you a range of values, depending on certain assumptions about your injuries. For instance, he may say, "Well, you banged your left knee, and it's swollen now. Your neck and back hurt. The fingers in both of your hands are numb. You could have some serious injuries. You'll probably need to get MRI scans of your neck, back, and knee. You'll also need neurological testing for carpal tunnel syndrome in your hands. If all of the tests are normal, and all you have are some bruises and sprains, and the treating doctors assign you a minimal permanent impairment rating, your case might be worth $5,000 to $10,000, and I might make a demand of $25,000.

"But if you have positive findings, like a herniated disc in your neck or back, or torn cartilage in your knee, your case could be worth $50,000 to $100,000, or much more than that if surgery is required. Plus, how much time you miss from work will be a factor and how much of your medical bills remains outstanding. So right now, it's hard to say exactly. We'll know more after we get all the doctors' reports."

That's a lot to digest, especially if this is your first conversation with a lawyer. But after four or five consultations, you'll start hearing some things repeated, and it will all make more and more sense to you.

One thing you will hear from all the lawyers is the need for medical reports. The opinions of doctors, and the results of diagnostic tests are major factors in evaluating injury cases. Going to the right doctor, or doctors, can help your case a lot, and going to the wrong ones can seriously hurt your case. This may seem unfair to you; perhaps, it may even seem dishonest. Why should the doctor make any difference when your injury is exactly the same regardless of who sees you, or what they say?

The fact is, however, most legal cases involve a battle of the experts. The injured person is the Plaintiff and the negligent person is the Defendant. The Plaintiff's doctors testify that the Plaintiff was seriously injured as the direct result of this accident. The Defendant's doctors testify that the Plaintiff is not very injured at all, or that most of the injuries existed before the accident.

The doctors on both sides believe they are testifying to the truth, as they see it. They are doing the best they can to interpret the medical facts to benefit whichever side is paying their bill. Medicine is not an exact science—if you have gone to three different doctors and received three different opinions about your illness, you know this is true. Generally, doctors (especially neurologists and orthopedic surgeons) fall into one of these groups: plaintiff-oriented, defense-oriented, or middle of the road.

Not only do doctors have different opinions when they examine you, their opinions can also differ when they interpret sophisticated diagnostic tests, such as an MRI scan. MRI stands for magnetic resonance imaging. It is one of the greatest advances in recent medicine. Scanning a specific part of the body with magnetic imaging allows doctors to see things that used to require exploratory surgery, or other invasive procedures such as myelograms. A myelogram involves a needle inserted into the base of the spine through which dye is injected into the fluid surrounding the nerves and spinal cord. The procedure can be painful, and it requires X-ray exposure. Possible aftereffects may include nausea and vomiting. The most common aftereffect is a headache that can last for days.

A standard X ray may only show a fracture, dislocation, curvature of the spine, or degenerative conditions such as arthritis. Remember when you went to the emergency room, and they took all those X rays, and they were all normal? You may still have serious injuries, such as herniated discs in the neck or back, or torn cartilage in the knee. These are the types of problems that can show up on MRI scans.

But the technology is growing so rapidly that an old, or less expensive MRI unit may fail to show a problem that is picked up by a more sophisticated unit. The technician who administers the scan and the doctors who read it may also vary in experience and ability, as well as in their inclination toward Plaintiff or Defense. Thus, four different doctors looking at an MRI film of the back may all say something different: from normal to bulge, protrusion to herniation. Still another may say it's herniated, but not from the accident.

Does it sound like your whole case is totally at the mercy of a group of doctors and what they write in their reports? To some extent, that is true. This brings us to the next question you must ask the lawyer in your initial consultation. What doctors should I see?

Over the years, I have attended many continuing legal education seminars on personal injury. I continue to be amazed at how many distinguished and reputable lawyers advise against referring a new client to a specific doctor or doctors. Their rationale is that, if the case goes to court, the jury will be adversely swayed when the Plaintiff admits that her lawyer referred her to her doctors. First of all, as I said in the introduction, most cases are settled without a lawsuit. Of the minority, where suit is filed, most of those are settled before a jury makes a decision. And in the small percentage where a jury is involved, the Plaintiff's lawyer can simply say to the jury, "My client came to me with a serious injury. She didn't know any doctors. She asked me to refer her to somebody who could help her. I referred her to doctors who are specialists in their field, with excellent reputations. They are board certified in their specialty. Would it have been better if I turned her away and told her to find her own doctors?"

In my opinion, a lawyer who refuses to refer his client to a doctor may be opening himself up to a possible malpractice claim, especially if the client ends up getting treatment from a doctor who turns out to be a regular "hired gun" of the insurance companies. Certainly, that lawyer is not taking good care of his client.

You ask the lawyer what doctors he would recommend. At this point, he may say that you would have to hire him as your lawyer before he will make doctor referrals. Again, you need to be up front with the lawyer right from the beginning, especially if you like him, and he's been patient and informative enough to answer your questions. Tell him (either on the phone or in person), "I'm not ready to hire any lawyer yet, although I like you a lot and may hire you in the future. But I do need medical treatment badly, and I want to be sure I go to the right doctors. If you give me the names of the doctors you trust, I'll mention to them that you referred me, if you want me to."

When a lawyer hears this, he may very well decide to go along with you. He still hopes to win you over as a client. For this reason, he will want you to see the doctors with whom he works, to ensure that your case will be handled properly from the medical side. He may also score some points with that doctor for referring you. The old saying "One hand washes the other" is certainly true in the legal and medical professions. Even if the lawyer doesn't end up getting you as a client, the doctor may refer a better case to him later on. Kickbacks of money are illegal and unethical (although there are lawyers and doctors who risk their careers doing it); however, reciprocity by referring new patients or clients is perfectly acceptable.

Depending on the injuries, there are different doctors you are likely to see. If your injury required stiches which will result in a permanent scar to a visible part of your body, you should see a plastic surgeon. For most injuries to the neck and back, you may see an orthopedic surgeon, or neurosurgeon, or a neurologist. These three specialists are medical doctors, and they may have within their offices a licensed physical therapist to treat you.

You may also be referred to a chiropractor, who will generally do some of the same things as a physical therapist (hot packs, ultrasound etc.), as well as doing adjustments or manipulations to the spine. Some people swear by chiropractors; others swear at them. From a legal standpoint, chiropractors are generally qualified to testify as experts and give opinions just like medical doctors. Usually, physical therapists can only testify as to what treatment they gave and are not qualified to render medical opinions.

Therefore, for neck and back injuries, I generally recommend a chiropractor for the regular treatment of a client, and an orthopedic surgeon and neurologist as consulting experts. These specialists will prescribe medication and recommend diagnostic testing, including the MRI scans we have discussed.

At the end of the case, when the client has been discharged, we will have three reports from doctors in three different specialties, all agreeing that my client has sustained a serious and permanent injury from the accident. We will discuss in a later chapter the important details of these reports, including the concept of permanent impairment.

For now, you need to be comparing notes from your free consultations. Are there one or two doctors that have been named by several lawyers? These may be the doctors you should see, as soon as possible. Lying in bed is not the answer. Hoping that your body will, in time, just heal itself naturally is not going to help you or your case.

Let's say you decide you are going to wait awhile, to see how you are doing. Before you know it, a month has gone by. You have been taking lots of nonprescription pain pills so you could function. You went back to work in a few days. You come home from work in constant pain, but you keep hoping it's going to get better. Finally, after a month of the pain getting worse, you decide you have to see a doctor. Here's what you have managed to do: you have seriously aggravated your condition by failing to get medical therapy and treatment, and by pushing yourself back to work too soon. In addition, you have significantly weakened your case, because the insurance company is sure to say, "Oh, come on, you couldn't have been hurt very badly or you would have seen a doctor a lot sooner." So do yourself, and your case, a favor—immediately schedule those appointments with a chiropractor, neurologist, and orthopedic surgeon. And don't go back to work until you have discussed it with your doctors, and until you really feel ready.

Summarized in Checklist III are some of the important questions you should ask in your free consultations.

Checklist III
(Questions to Ask in Free Legal Consultations)

1. What is the law in your state regarding use of uninsured motorist coverage and stacking?
2. Regarding claims evaluation, what does the lawyer know about the other driver's insurance company and your own?
3. What are the best car insurance companies for high evaluation and prompt payment of claims?
4. What is the statute of limitations in your state?
5. What is the lawyer's contingency fee, and how is it determined?
6. Does the lawyer ask you for costs up front, and does he charge for office overhead costs?
7. What is the value of your case?
8. What doctors should you see?

CHAPTER 4

Going to the Doctors and Getting the Bills Paid

It has been two weeks since the accident. By this time, you should be seeing your chiropractor regularly. You should also have had one appointment with the orthopedic surgeon and neurologist, or at least have appointments scheduled. These treating doctors should be the ones whose names came up most often in your initial free consultations with the lawyers.

Incidentally, you should try to clarify payment of the doctors' bills at your first appointment. Most doctors like to be paid up front, regardless of insurance. However, if your treating doctors handle a lot of personal injury cases and accept referrals from lawyers, they should be willing to bill the insurance companies so you don't have to pay. Let's assume that your car insurance pays for 80 percent of your bills, and your group health insurance coverage pays the other 20 percent. Try to get each doctor to agree to accept whatever your two insurance companies pay. If they do agree, get it in writing.

The chiropractor should be the most flexible about billing, and also the most convenient to book appointments. You may have already returned to work, or are about to do so. Chiropractors generally will try to get you in either before or after work, and perhaps on Saturday or Sunday. You also should be able to find a good chiropractor close to where you live or work. Hopefully, your first visit to the chiropractor was within a few days after the accident.

Most chiropractors will offer various types of therapy, many of which are similar or identical to what you would receive from a licensed physical therapist. These treatments include hot packs, ultrasound, and massage. Some chiropractors may have a licensed massage therapist on their staff, or one who comes to the office on a regular basis for their patients. Some chiropractors may also offer acupuncture.

In addition, chiropractors have been trained to do spinal adjustments or manipulations. Many people, even if they have never been in an accident, go to chiropractors on a regular basis to be adjusted. If you've suffered a severe sprain or strain in the accident, your condition should gradually improve with time and the combination of treatments from the chiropractor. Every individual responds differently to treatment.

It is very important that you communicate clearly with your chiropractor. Tell him what feels good and what doesn't, what is working and what isn't. Some people feel that spinal adjustments help them a lot; others feel much worse after them. Remember, you are the patient. It's your body. Take some responsibility for your own treatment.

Certainly, after a couple of weeks, you'll have a good feel for the types of treatment you prefer. If something is really hurting you more than helping, discuss this with the chiropractor. He should be open and flexible enough to work with you; after all, his primary concern should be your well-being and improvement. If he is inflexible and totally ignores your requests, you should switch chiropractors.

Chiropractors are taught to help the body heal itself naturally. They are neither trained, nor legally authorized to prescribe medications. For pain pills, muscle relaxers, cortisone shots, and the like, you will need medical doctors. You probably received some prescriptions at the emergency room. You should have filled these prescriptions and submitted the bills to your insurance company for reimbursement. Incidentally, you should also be keeping track of your mileage to the doctors' offices. You may be able to get reimbursed directly from your insurance company, or at least include these expenses as part of your claim later on, against the other insurance company.

For your types of injuries, which include pain and trauma to the head, neck, back, knee, and hand, it is essential that you have thorough evaluations by an orthopedic surgeon and neurologist. These doctors can renew or change your prescriptions. More importantly, they should be able to diagnose any serious injury beyond a sprain or strain. You hit your left knee during the accident. It still is slightly swollen, and you continue to feel a dull pain. It also seems to make a cracking sound occasionally and gives way on you once in a while. It is very possible you have suffered some internal derangement to your knee, such as torn cartilage. This type of problem would not show up on an X ray, but may be seen on an MRI scan.

Your neck and lower back continue to hurt you constantly, even though the chiropractor's treatment seems to give you some temporary relief. You have never had a problem before with your neck or back and you're worried. You are also getting headaches with pain that seems to shoot up from the back of your neck. You have never had headaches like this before. The X rays are all negative. Again, the MRI scans may show a herniated, protruding, or bulging disc.

The chiropractor might also try to refer you for an MRI. Generally, it is advisable to go to the MRI referred by the orthopedic surgeon or neurologist. The MRI is usually interpreted by a radiologist who will then review his findings with the referring doctor. A neurologist or orthopedic surgeon, in conjunction with the radiologist, is usually better qualified than the chiropractor to read the MRI films.

Be aware that each doctor is also likely to have a financial interest in a certain MRI center. He may either own a piece of the center, or get some type of referral fee for each patient he sends. Florida and some other states are passing laws to force doctors to give up their financial interests in diagnostic centers. Abuses do occur frequently where unnecessary diagnostic tests, including

MRI scans, are routinely given, solely for the doctor's financial gain.

With this knowledge, you can take some control in determining which tests you will undergo. Your own limited insurance coverage may force you to make some hard choices. Let's say you have a total of $10,000 in Personal Injury Protection benefits. This pays for 80 percent of your medical bills, and 60 percent of your lost wages. You might use up $1,500 for lost wages. You want to make the best use of the $8,500 that's left for medical bills. An MRI scan for one part of the body may cost $1,000 to $1,500, or even more, if multiple views are required. The doctors may recommend scans for your head, back, neck, and left knee. If you had all four, you would have used up $5,000 to $6,000 of your medical coverage. That doesn't leave much for your visits to the chiropractor, three or four times a week, or for the orthopedic surgeon, neurologist, and emergency room with all those X rays.

The neurologist will also be concerned about the tingling and numbness in your fingers and hands. This could be a sign of carpal tunnel syndrome, an injury to the median nerve which passes through a tunnel in the center of the wrist. This area is particularly vulnerable to trauma if the wrist is extended. Remember when your hands were jammed against the steering wheel at the moment of impact?

The neurologist will recommend a series of expensive diagnostic tests, including electro-myelogram (EMG). An EMG is a technique to determine nerve injury such as carpal tunnel syndrome. The EMG involves electrical pulses to various nerves of the arms and legs. Simultaneously, the neurologist uses a needle to probe various muscles and to measure electrical patterns.

If you undergo every single test, your benefits will soon be exhausted. Of course, your group insurance from work can then start paying 80 percent of the bills. But remember, you may have to pay back your group insurance company out of your settlement. So, if you want to cut down those expensive bills, at least a little, then discuss with your doctors which tests are most critical. Your input is important, and *you* will make the final decision, *not* the doctor.

If your headaches are almost gone, forget about the MRI of the brain. If your main neurological complaint is the tingling and numbness in your fingers, just do the EMG, and not the other neurological tests. If your neck, back, and knee are all still hurting, then get MRIs of those three areas. The MRI of the knee may show torn cartilage. The neck and back MRI scans may indicate herniations. The EMG would confirm carpal tunnel syndrome.

If you have any positive test results, the value of your case has skyrocketed. When the insurance adjuster sees these results, he'll have to change his evaluation from a $5,000 sprain case, to one worth $50,000 to $100,000 or more. But you can bet he'll start out offering you a lot less.

CHAPTER 5

Speaking to the Insurance Adjuster

A month has gone by. Your visits to the chiropractor have gone from three to four times a week, to twice a week. You have seen the neurologist and orthopedic surgeon twice each. You have had MRI scans and an EMG. You have returned to work. You have had free phone consultations with several attorneys and have seen a couple of them personally. You should now have a good idea about the laws in your state regarding car accidents. You should also know what your insurance covers and what changes you need to make for the future.

In addition, you have obtained the accident report, which gives the information about the other driver and his insurance company. If the owner of the other vehicle is different than the driver, the owner's name and address will also be listed. If you have not yet heard from the insurance company of the other driver, or owner, it is time for you to make a move.

As we previously discussed, you can determine the phone number of the other insurance company through the 800 directory assistance, your phone directory, if they have a local office, or you can ask your own insurance agent or the adjuster from your own company. They may have already contacted the other company. Sometimes you will not have to do anything on your own; the other insurance company's adjuster will contact you as soon as he has the file. He will probably want to take your recorded statement, either over the phone or personally.

If you are represented by an attorney, this statement would generally be done in your lawyer's office. Your lawyer would prepare you ahead of time by rehearsing many of the questions that you are likely to be asked. Your lawyer would also be present, to interrupt if he felt any questions were improper, or try to guide you, if he sensed you were in trouble. However, since you are doing this on your own, you have some decisions to make.

There is no legal requirement that you voluntarily give your statement to the other insurance company. The only time you would be required to do so would be if there were a lawsuit filed, and you were subpoenaed for your deposition. Therefore, you do have the choice of refusing to cooperate with the adjuster. You can tell him that you have had consultations with lawyers who have advised you against giving your statement, at least until you are represented by counsel.

If you are the kind of person who gets nervous easily, forgets or confuses things, and generally makes an unfavorable impression, you may choose to avoid giving your statement. However, if you are this type of person, you may be better off allowing an attorney to handle your case right from the beginning to avoid all of the anxiety and aggravation that may lie ahead. You may also wish to avoid giving your statement if you are easily irritated, short tempered, or generally obnoxious (you know yourself a lot better than I do).

However, if you are a sincere, honest, pleasant, likeable person, it will definitely be to your advantage to allow the adjuster to take your statement personally. First impressions are always very important. The insurance adjuster will be aware not only of what you are saying, but also how you are saying it.

The adjuster will be trying to make a determination on what lawyers call your "credibility." Credibility basically means will a jury empathize with you and believe you? You are a hard working school teacher, devoted wife, and mother of two with no previous injuries or prior accident claims. Just be yourself, and the insurance adjuster will realize that you are a very credible lady, whose claim he is going to make every effort to settle.

Understand, however, that his job is to settle the claim as quickly and cheaply as possible. Most insurance adjusters have what they call a "local limit." This means that they have a certain amount of authority to settle every case assigned to them, without seeking authorization from others, including claims committees and home offices. Most adjusters will investigate a claim and make a report to their supervisor. The supervisor will authorize the adjuster to settle for a certain amount up to his maximum authority, which could be $5,000, $10,000, or more depending on the particular company and the type of case.

If an insurance adjuster can settle the claim quickly for far less than his maximum authority, he will happily do so. There are some insurance adjusters that genuinely care about the injured claimants, especially if the injury is very serious. But even the most caring insurance adjuster still owes his primary duty to his employer, the insurance company. The more cheaply a case can be settled, the greater profit the insurance company will earn.

Therefore, if the insurance adjuster decides to make you an offer after taking your statement, you can assume that it is a lowball figure, and your case is worth substantially more. As I discussed earlier, it is really impossible to properly evaluate a case until you have concluded your medical treatment and have final reports with permanent impairment ratings from one or more doctors. The insurance adjuster, if he makes an unsolicited offer to settle at this stage, will be assuming that all of your medical reports and diagnostic tests are negative. The figure he will be offering you will, almost certainly, be much less than you can get after obtaining favorable doctor reports, or positive diagnostic tests.

If he asks you how much you want to settle your case, you should definitely not commit yourself to any figure, even if you think it is a high one. Once you state a specific amount, you will be setting the ceiling on your case, regardless of what subsequent medical treatment, diagnostic tests, and doctor reports indicate.

Let's say that you think you'd be happy with a settlement of $10,000, so you figure it can't hurt to tell the adjuster you would settle for $20,000 right now. The adjuster now knows that $20,000 is your top figure, and that he should be able to settle with you for substantially less. If it turns out that you have a more serious problem than you realize, and that your case may really be worth $40,000 or $50,000, there is no way that you are ever going to get more than $20,000 without getting involved in a lawsuit. You have also substantially weakened your case in the event of a lawsuit, since that $20,000 figure will be permanently a part of the insurance company's file.

Now the insurance adjuster asks, "How much do you want to settle your case?" You should respond, "How much are you willing to offer me?" That puts the ball in his lap, and you have not committed yourself to any figure or hurt yourself in any way. If he does give you a figure, you know that your case is going to be worth much more than that. Whatever figure he gives you then becomes part of your own file, as a starting point for future reference.

You can then tell him, "No. I am not interested. Right now my primary concern is in getting better and getting proper medical treatment for my injuries. I am considering getting an attorney, but until I do so, you can speak to me directly."

Let's get back to the preparation for giving the statement to the adjuster. There are some general rules that we always discuss with our clients before any statement or deposition. If you don't remember something, say, "I don't remember." Otherwise, if you try to guess, and you are wrong, your credibility will be adversely affected. Likewise, if you don't know something, say, "I don't know." If the question relates to a period of time, and you know the approximate time, you can just say, "I don't know exactly, but it was approximately the last week of November"; or say "approximately one week after the accident." However, if you cannot even give an approximation, it is better to just say, "I don't remember" or "I don't know."

Be sure to listen carefully to each question before answering. If the question simply calls for a yes or no, do not elaborate. Let the adjuster do the work. The only exception to this relates to any question involving your complaints, problems, or injuries as a result of the accident. If he asks you "What is bothering you now?", you should go on in as much detail as possible, as long as you are honest and sincere. An open-ended question like this also will allow you to explain how the accident has affected your life. You should consider discussing how it has limited you in work, as well as your marital and family life, and recreational activities.

However, be aware of the distinct possibility of surveillance. It is not unusual for insurance companies to have a photographer or investigator taking videotapes of you engaging in various activities. The worse thing you can do is testify that you have been unable to do something since the accident, if, in fact, you have been doing that activity.

For example, you may say, "I used to enjoy gardening in my backyard before the accident, but I can't do that anymore, because it hurts my back." One month later, you find out that there is a video showing you bending up and down, while weeding your vegetable garden. Remember, you must be truthful. Perhaps you are attempting to continue gardening, but have only been doing so in pain. This is what you must state.

Or you might say, "I used to play very competitive singles tennis, but now I can only play social doubles, and I do so with a lot of pain." Then, when they have the surveillance film showing you playing doubles, you can say, "Yes, I told you I am trying to play doubles, but that day I was really hurting and suffered quite a bit for days afterwards."

The key use of video surveillance is not so much to show you doing physical things; rather, it is to impeach your credibility—to make you out to be a liar. As long as you are consistent, honest, and sincere in your statements, video surveillance cannot hurt you. Just use your common sense when it comes to deciding what physical activities you should continue to pursue and to what degree. Remember, your body has been injured and is in a vulnerable position. You are much more likely to aggravate your injury if you attempt to do too much too soon.

The adjuster is also quite likely to ask you about previous injuries and accident claims, and prior medical treatment. A good insurance adjuster (and defense attorney, if the case goes to court) will be looking for a prior injury or previous medical condition similar to the injury you are claiming occurred from this accident. Their goal, of course, is to show that you really had the problem before the accident. Therefore, the accident either changed nothing, or, at most, merely aggravated your pre-existing condition.

Again, you must be totally honest regarding his questions. Do not even think about attempting to conveniently forget an old accident claim. The insurance companies have access to a computerized network which will bring up every claim you have made against insurance companies, even if it only involved property damage. You must be sure to mention any such claim and then clarify it as necessary.

For example, you might say, "Back some time in 1986, I was rear-ended; however, I was not injured. The other driver's insurance company paid for the damage to my car."

Or you might say, "About six years ago, I slipped and fell in a Sears store and hurt my left shoulder; however, that was my only injury. Right now, it is my neck and back that are hurting from this accident. I never had any previous problems with my neck or back."

If you have had previous treatment to any part of your body which has been injured from this accident, again you must be truthful about it. Even if it was not from an accident, the insurance company can find out about it sooner or later.

If you are unable to settle your case on your own, and a lawsuit must be filed, one of the first things you will have to do is answer a written set of questions called interrogatories. This will almost always include a question asking you to list all doctors you have seen over the last five or ten years. A good defense attorney will get the medical records of all of those doctors and sift through hundreds of pages to find treatment for the parts of your body injured from this accident. If you previously testified you had no problems with these areas, you have seriously and permanently ruined your credibility. Again, your goal should be to answer honestly, and to clarify your answer in a light as favorable to you as possible.

For example, you can say, "I did have a minor back problem a few years ago after playing a hard tennis match. I saw Dr. Smith, a chiropractor in town, a few times a week for a couple of months, and then I felt fine. I haven't had any problems or needed any treatment since then." When the adjuster follows up with that doctor, the records will indicate that you were discharged with no further symptoms.

Once the adjuster gets by the background questions on your previous medical condition and prior accident claims, he will get into the questions relating to how the accident happened. In your case, you were stopped at a traffic light and were rear-ended. This is quite simple and straightforward.

Other cases and situations may not be as clear. The adjuster may attempt to uncover statements from you which will make it appear that you were at least partially at fault for the accident. For example, let's assume that the light was green, and you were proceeding through the intersection. Suddenly, somebody makes a left turn directly in front of you, failing to yield the right of way. You attempt to swerve, but it is too late, and you hit the side of the other car.

This is generally considered to be a case of clear liability against the other driver, since you had the right of way. Any driver making a left-hand turn must wait for all oncoming traffic to clear before proceeding. However, a good adjuster will try to ask questions leading to the conclusion that you should have been able to avoid the turning car; therefore, to some degree the accident was your fault.

The adjuster could ask you these types of questions: "How fast were you going through the intersection before the collision?" "How far away was the other car when you first saw it?" "How many seconds elapsed between the time you first saw the other car and the time you hit it?" "If you had that much time, why weren't you able to swerve around to either side to avoid the collision?"

Depending on your answer to each question, a good adjuster will follow it up with a more difficult question, attempting to allow you to dig yourself further and further into a hole.

If you find yourself under this type of questioning, remember to go back to our basic rules. Listen to the question first. If it calls for a yes or no answer, do not volunteer anything else. If you do not know, or do not remember, state that you don't, rather than guessing and getting yourself into further trouble. If you answer, "I don't remember" three or four consecutive times, it will frustrate even the most clever adjuster.

If there were any witnesses to your accident and their names and addresses appear on the accident report, you should make every effort to contact them as soon as possible and find out what they will be saying. In a disputed liability case, an independent witness can make or break your case. If you know the witness will be favorable to you, you can just refer the adjuster to that witness, and say that the witness remembers the accident better than you do.

However, if you feel confident and very clear about all of the facts of the accident, and you answer the questions truthfully and with great conviction, you will have established yourself as a credible person whose testimony cannot be shaken. Again, you know yourself and your demeanor best. If you really are not sure about some of the occurrences that led up to the accident, it is much better to say you don't remember. However, if it is absolutely clear in your mind, and you can express that clarity in your statement, then do so. Remember, though, to only answer the adjuster's question and not volunteer anything beyond that.

The questions relating to how the accident occurred, and what happened immediately before and after will take up the largest part of the statement. After that, the adjuster will probably only ask you a few questions relating to what medical treatment you had following the accident and the nature of your injuries. Prior to your statement being taken, you should review all of your doctors' bills. You should also ask your doctors for copies of their records, and review everything the doctors said.

By the way, this brings up another point regarding your

previous medical history. Almost every doctor will either ask you directly about your previous medical history, or have you fill out a form in his office. Just as you must be totally honest with the adjuster regarding any past problems, the same is true of any doctor that you see. The important thing is consistency. As long as each doctor gets the same medical history, and this is the history you discuss with the adjuster, there will be no room for doubt.

Therefore, it is important that you obtain the doctors' reports or records as soon as possible, to be sure that the past history is accurate. If there are any mistakes, you should point these out to the doctor, immediately, so that he can correct his records. The doctors' bills and records will also help you in answering the questions about dates of treatment following the accident. You can ask the adjuster to allow you to have these bills and records in front of you when you are giving the statement. You can also give a copy of the bills and reports to the adjuster, who may not yet have everything that you have.

You can say, "Here are Dr. Jones's and Dr. Smith's bills and reports. They show the dates that I was there and the problems that I was having." However, do not miss the opportunity to complain about all of your present complaints and limitations. The doctors' records are only going to indicate some of your major problems and will not go into the kind of detail that you will be allowed on your statement.

The adjuster may, or may not ask you if you have anything to add before he concludes the statement. If he does ask you this, and you have not had the chance to express all of your present complaints and limitations, take this opportunity to do so. If he doesn't ask you that, you are entitled to ask him to allow you to speak. You can end the statement with a clear picture of how this accident has affected your normal life.

If you have lost time from work, you can give him copies of your previous pay stubs so that it is clear how much you were earning at the time of the accident. Be sure you know the exact dates you missed from work. Even if you were paid during your absence, it is important to bring out your lost time to show that you were hurt seriously enough to be unable to work. Also, you are entitled to claim, as part of your damages, lost vacation or sick leave time.

Are you still out of work? Have your injuries affected your ability to properly do your job? It is very important to discuss these issues. Your future loss of earning capacity could be a major part of your claim, especially if you have to look for another type of work as a result of this accident.

The adjuster will most likely make a tape recording of your statement. Be sure to state on the tape that you want a copy of the tape and a copy of any transcription.

When the statement is concluded, you can ask the adjuster about any claim for which you are still awaiting payment such as property damage, car rental reimbursement, prescription reimbursement, or payment of doctor bills. Depending on your state's laws and the insurance coverage, this adjuster may or may not be responsible for some of those payments. If he is not responsible, he may be able to tell you who is.

If your statement went well, this may be the time when the adjuster tries to feel you out to see if you are willing to make a quick settlement. Remember what we discussed earlier; do not commit yourself to any specific figure, but do not hesitate to ask him to make you an offer.

If he does make you an offer, think of it as a card game, and keep a poker face. If he says, "I'll give you $20,000," and you would have been happy with $5,000 or $10,000, don't show him your excitement. Remember, whatever offer he makes, will be a lowball figure. You can be sure that there is more where that came from.

If he tries to put the ball back in your corner and says, "I can't make you an offer until you tell me what you want," you must remain noncommittal. Just tell him, "It's too early for me to commit myself. I don't know yet how serious my injuries are, or how much additional medical treatment I might require." Be courteous and friendly. Thank him for taking the time to be with you, and leave the door open for further communication.

One more thing that should have been mentioned earlier—

you can insist that the statement be taken in your home, where you feel most comfortable. This will allow you to make the best impression and have the adjuster see you as you really are—a warm, honest, friendly, person who has been wrongfully injured through no fault of your own. You may have your family around you for support and encouragement. Just be yourself, and you'll do fine.

CHAPTER 6

Final Exams

It's been five months since the accident. You've had MRI scans of your neck, back, and knee, and an EMG. You're down to once-a-week visits with the chiropractor. You have seen the neurologist and orthopedic surgeon about once a month. On your last visit to each of them, the doctors said you may be discharged on your next visit. You are approaching what the doctors and lawyers call "maximum medical improvement," or "M.M.I." This means that you have reached a plateau. You're not going to get much better with continued treatment. You're still having some problems.

Your knee is doing much better. The MRI of the knee was normal. The MRI scans of your back and neck showed bulging discs, but no herniations. A bulge is considered an abnormal finding, but it is not that serious. Since you had no previous back or neck problems, the neurologist and orthopedic surgeon may be willing to state in their reports that the bulging discs were the direct result of the accident. You should be sure to discuss this opinion with them, because their view on causation is important to your case.

Remember that whatever they say, it is only their opinion.

As sophisticated as the MRI scans may be, they are not like the rings on a tree. They cannot pinpoint the exact date of a bulging or herniated disc. That's why your previous history is so important. When doctors give their opinion in the legal system, it is based upon "reasonable medical probability." In other words, your doctors will be saying that it's more likely, or probable, that the bulging discs are from the accident, since you had no problems before.

Likewise, the insurance company will want their own doctors to review the MRI films. Their doctors are paid to say whatever will be helpful to the insurance company. Naturally, the opinion must have some reasonable medical basis. With MRI interpretations, just about anything is possible. I've seen reports from insurance company doctors that say any of the following:

1. There is no bulging disc. The MRI is totally normal.
2. This is not a bulging disc, but a congenital abnormality (in other words, you were born with it).
3. There is a mild bulging disc, but it could not be from the accident, because the MRI was taken too soon and the arthritis shown would have taken longer to develop;
4. The bulging disc couldn't be from the accident, because no arthritis is shown, and it would have formed already;
5. There is no bulge, only the early stages of a degenerative condition which is normal for a thirty-seven-year-old woman.

As you can see, the cause of your injury becomes a matter of one opinion against another. On the cases that do go to court, it is up to the jury to decide by "the greater weight of the evidence" what your damages really are. Civil cases, unlike criminal matters, do not need to be proven "beyond a reasonable doubt." As a Plaintiff, you only have to tip the scales to 51 percent in your favor.

Therefore, if your doctors have good reputations, and can express themselves clearly and credibly, you have a good chance of winning. So don't worry if the insurance adjuster sends you a copy of his doctor's report which basically says that your doctors' opinions are hogwash.

You are still getting a little tingling and numbness in both hands. The EMG done by your neurologist indicates a mild, bilateral carpal tunnel syndrome. We have already explained carpal tunnel syndrome. Bilateral means that both hands are affected. Your neurologist says it's not serious enough to consider surgery, but it could get worse with time. The insurance company doctor who reviewed the EMG actually agrees completely with that diagnosis and opinion. This fact will be very important when you begin to negotiate your settlement in the near future.

Your medical bills to date total $11,500. So far, your car insurance PIP coverage has paid 80 percent. But your insurance company is getting tired of paying the bills. You just got a notice from your company saying they want you to see Dr. C. U. Toff in two weeks for an "independent medical examination." As you can tell from this doctor's fictitious name, he is likely to "cut off" your benefits by saying you don't need any further treatment. However, if you refuse to see him, your insurance company will cut off your benefits anyway, for failing to cooperate under the policy.

This puts you in a no-win situation. You can try to buy a little extra time by rescheduling the appointment. Perhaps the doctor's office is too far away from where you live and work. Request a different doctor closer to you. Maybe you weren't given enough notice, and you can't get that time off from work. Perhaps you're really going to be out of town that day.

Your insurance company will usually accept a legitimate excuse and reschedule at least once. Meanwhile, you can let your treating doctors know about the Independent Medical Examination (IME). They may be able to move up your discharge date so their final visits will occur before your insurance company examination. That way, when you do get cut off, all your bills will have already been paid.

Even if you can't arrange for all of your treatment to conclude before your IME, you should avoid going. It's better to be cut off without an adverse doctor's opinion on the record. The other insurance company, from whom you hope to get your settlement, can easily find out about your IME results and use that against you in negotiations. Besides, if any of your final bills are not paid by your car insurance, you can submit them to your group health insurance carrier. The worst thing that could happen would be that your group carrier will want some of the money back from the settlement; this is called a subrogation lien (see chapter 10).

Now, let's assume you have been able to make appointments with the orthopedic surgeon and neurologist for final examinations before your Personal Injury Protection cutoff date (the date scheduled for your IME.) Your chiropractor says he would like to treat you for a few more weeks, but he'll "work out" any outstanding bill with you. What do you need to know about these final examinations?

All through your treatment, you should have been telling your doctors exactly what's been hurting you. In the final examination, it's particularly important to emphasize your present complaints. When the doctor goes through your normal range of motion (moving your neck, bending, lifting your leg, etc.), you must stop as soon as you feel any pain or discomfort. Restriction in the range of motion is an important factor when the doctor evaluates your permanent impairment.

Remind your doctor about the ways this accident has affected your normal life. You used to work out in aerobics class three evenings a week and play tennis on the weekends. You have been unable to do any of that since the accident. You can't pick up your three-year-old, something you used to do all the time. Your body is aching by the end of the school day. And because of your carpal tunnel syndrome, you have trouble picking up and holding objects. Your fingers are always tingling. This also keeps you up at night. Don't lie or exaggerate about anything, but do be honest and thorough. Ask your doctor his opinion regarding restrictions on your normal activities. Some of your discussion will find its way to his final report.

Also, discuss with him the fact that the chiropractor's treatments do provide you with some relief, and ask if he can recommend some continued treatment. This will allow you to argue, in your upcoming negotiations, that you will have significant future medical bills, some of which will have to be paid out of your pocket. This will be especially true once your PIP benefits are exhausted or terminated since you won't be attending your impending Independent Medical exam by bad old Dr. C. U. Toff.

By the way, how do you go about getting out of that appointment with Dr. C. U. Toff? A few days before the IME date, call your insurance adjuster, say you've been discharged by two of your three doctors, and you simply don't wish to attend the appointment. The adjuster will act very upset and tell you that your benefits will be terminated. Remember, now, this is the adjuster for your company, not the other company with whom you will shortly begin settlement negotiations. Your benefits are just about exhausted anyway. Your group insurance through work may pick up some of the chiropractor's additional bills, and he has told you he will "work out" any outstanding bills. So, you really don't need your company anymore. Just tell him you'll expect payment on the final exams from the orthopedic surgeon and neurologist, which were scheduled prior to your IME date. The company is legally obligated to pay all bills incurred until the date the IME is cancelled. Your company will send you a nasty letter, telling you how terrible you are for not going to their hatchet man. Your carrier will then regretfully inform you that your benefits are cut off, as of the day of the IME (the exam that never was).

Ask to get the final "payout sheet," which lists amounts of all doctors' bills, dates incurred, and dates paid. You can then use this payout sheet, and the letter terminating benefits when you submit future bills to your group insurance company. Your group may pay some portion of the outstanding bills, depending on what's in your policy. But, as we mentioned earlier, your group carrier may want its money back (subrogation lien) from your settlement. However, we'll deal with that when you get that super offer; the one that's too good to refuse, but you do.

CHAPTER 7

Playing the Game of Negotiating

You have just received the final ingredient in your recipe for success—your doctors' final reports. These reports are the key to the value of your case. Hopefully, the orthopedic surgeon, neurologist, and chiropractor have assigned permanent impairment ratings. Perhaps the orthopedic surgeon, who may be the most conservative of the three, has given you a "10 percent permanent impairment to the body as a whole" pursuant to the American Medical Association's guidelines. In layman's terms, this means you are only 90 percent as good as you used to be. But, in the minds of lawyers and insurance adjusters, it means you've got a permanent injury. And that means you can argue that you're going to have these problems for the rest of your life. The standard mortality tables, which are commonly used by the lawyers and insurance companies, say you have forty-four years to live. That's 16,060 days you'll be living with pain. How much is that worth?

Let's say your neurologist gives you a 15 percent permanent impairment rating to the body as a whole. "Body as a whole" just means your whole body is affected. If you had just broken an arm and had no other injuries, the permanent impairment would be to "the upper extremity." The neurologist is concerned about your carpal tunnel syndrome. Although you don't need it now, he says you may require surgery if your symptoms get worse.

Your chiropractor, who is expected to be the most liberal of the three doctors, gives you a 20 percent permanent impairment to the body as a whole. He talks about numerous positive findings based on tests with strange names.

The bottom line is that all three doctors agree you have got a permanent problem. Now comes the fun part—starting settlement negotiations. But where do you start? How much do you ask for? How much is your case worth?

Well, you could go back to those lawyers for another free consultation. But they're not likely to be very cooperative at this point, because they're going to realize you're trying to settle on your own. I'm going to recommend saving them for a time down the road, when you may really need each other. There is another way to get the ball rolling, without giving up anything or weakening your negotiating position. Lawyers and adjusters call it the "policy limit demand."

Remember when we discussed the coverage amounts on the different insurance policies? In the example we gave, the guy who hit you has a liability policy limit of $50,000. Most of the time, the limits of the other driver will be anywhere from $10,000 to $100,000. No matter how serious your injuries are, the insurance company is never going to voluntarily give you more than its limits. So, what have you got to lose by starting out asking for the maximum?

You can use the sample demand letter at the end of this chapter, and adjust it to the particular facts of your case. Since the doctors' reports speak for themselves, you do not need to spend a lot of time quoting medical terminology you may not even understand. The adjuster is going to read all the reports anyway. The main thing he'll look at in your demand letter is *the bottom line*—how much are you asking? When he sees it's a policy limit demand, he'll already be thinking about how much he can save his company by settling for less than the limits.

An important part of the demand letter includes the section explaining how the accident has affected your life. This will help personalize your claim. The adjuster with whom you will be negotiating may be different than the one who took your recorded statement a few months ago. Even if he's the same guy, he will have forgotten you by now. The statement he took probably was mostly concerned with how the accident happened, any immediate medical care, and any previous accidents or pre-existing injuries.

The main purpose of the lifestyle portion of the demand letter is to explain in detail all of the things you used to do before the accident that you can't do now, or can only do in pain and with limitations. Perhaps you were an "A" singles player at your tennis club, and now you're reduced to playing "B" doubles. Maybe you worked out in an aerobics class three times a week, and now you're only walking a slow mile. Or, you used to roll around the floor and wrestle with your dog, and now you can only pet him. Make the examples specific and personalized. Most important, be truthful.

If the chiropractor discharged you but recommended follow-up care when needed, continue to go to him when you're in pain. Send those bills to the adjuster with the demand letter, and continue to send additional bills while the adjuster is in the process of evaluating your case. Be sure to give him a time limit to respond; thirty days is usually quite reasonable. If there's no time limit, your file will go to the bottom of his heap. A typical adjuster could have between 50 and 300 cases assigned to him. Therefore, he must work on them in priority order. If you tell him you're going to hire a lawyer if you don't hear from him in thirty days, he's going to make an extra effort to respond. He will definitely be motivated to settle the case without a lawyer involved.

When the adjuster makes a counteroffer, it will usually be by mail or phone. Lately, we've been getting more offers by FAX, so include your FAX number in your demand. But send the letter certified mail, return receipt requested. The thirty-day period will begin on the day that the green slip says the insurance company received it.

Three weeks later, you get "the call." The adjuster will probably start out with a typical casual greeting like "How are you?" But remember, this is not a casual conversation. Take notes on everything you both say. Record the conversation if at all possible. If he says "How are you?" tell him what's been bothering you that day, or that week. If the tingling in your right hand (from the carpal tunnel syndrome) has been getting worse since you sent the demand letter, let him know.

After the small talk, the adjuster, if he's smart, will probably say something like this:

"You've asked us for our $50,000 policy limits. Come on now, you know that's not realistic. What can we really settle this case for, right now?"

In the business, this is known as an attempt to force you to "bid against yourself." He's trying to make you come down from your policy limit demand, but he's not offering you *anything* in return. The most important rule of negotiating is *never* give up something without getting something in return. A corollary to this rule is try to get something for nothing.

So how do you answer the adjuster? Remember, everything you say in this conversation is vitally important. A good adjuster will read between the lines. He'll be interpreting what you say, how you say it, and what you don't say. Let's try three different responses to his question. Which one would you pick?

1. "I don't want to bid against myself. Make me an offer."
2. "I won't settle this case right now, unless you offer me the $50,000."
3. "You're right—$50,000 is not realistic, because my right hand is bothering me more than ever. If it stays like this, I'm going to need surgery for carpal tunnel syndrome. If the policy were higher, I'd have asked for more."

Did you pick answer number one? This would be the second best of the three answers. The best part of this answer is that it forces the adjuster to make a counteroffer, which is what you want. You've put the ball squarely back in his court. However, you are violating the most important rule of negotiating: you are giving up something for nothing. How? By saying "make me an offer," you are implying that you are willing to take less, that your bottom line is definitely under $50,000. Of course, you want him to make a counteroffer. But you want to get that counteroffer without giving up anything.

Answer number two certainly is forceful. But it is by far the worst of the three possibilities. Remember, your goal is to get a counteroffer without tipping your hand. If you say you won't take less than the $50,000, you've backed yourself into a no-win situation. You know the adjuster isn't going to just say, "Fine, here's the $50,000 policy limits—you win." So, if you give answer number two, it won't help you get the $50,000.

But, since you're saying you won't take less, the adjuster has no reason to offer you less. So he's likely to say, "Well, I guess there's nothing more to talk about. You'd better get a lawyer. We'll see you in court." You have just scared him away. You have accomplished nothing and received nothing. Worse, you've forced yourself into a lawyer's office, where you'll be completely at his mercy. In addition, answer number two isn't truthful, since you might consider settling for less than the $50,000, to avoid attorney's fees and costs.

This brings us to the best response, answer number three. The answer is truthful. You're re-emphasizing the strongest part of your case—the possibility of surgery if your hand gets worse. It is also true that if the policy limits were higher, you would have asked for more. Remember, the general strategy is to start out asking for the maximum. Answer number three, however, does not scare away the adjuster. You're not saying you won't take less. You're just saying you would have asked for more, if there was any more there. You haven't given up anything. You have strengthened your position and still left open the door for the counteroffer you really want.

Okay, let's assume you have given answer number three. The adjuster senses the time is right to negotiate. Here's what he says:

"Well, I do sympathize with your continuing problems, but none of the doctors have recommended surgery at this point. It's just a possibility, and the law doesn't recognize possibilities as part of your damages. You could wait for a year or two and see what happens. But if you want to get this over with right now, I can offer you $15,000. That's a lot of money, especially since almost all of your bills have been paid by your insurance company. And you don't have to give any of it to a lawyer. It's all yours, tax-free."

After all those months of going to doctors' offices, hassling with the insurance companies, getting all the medical records and reports, going through X rays, MRI scans, the EMG and months of chiropractic treatment, you've finally got something to show for it. You have already saved yourself about $5,000, based on the typical attorney's fee of one-third of any recovery without a lawsuit. Remember, most attorneys take their percentage off the top. Then they will deduct their costs and your outstanding bills. You'll get what's left.

Let's go back to the adjuster's counteroffer. Analyze his language when he offers you the $15,000. Sometimes, adjusters will say, "I'm not going to nickel and dime you. My maximum authority is $15,000." In this case, he simply said, "I can offer you $15,000." This implies that he's got more, that $15,000 is not his maximum authority.

What do you do next? Whatever you do, *don't* accept the $15,000 on the spot. Don't ever be afraid of losing what's already been offered by saying no. The only time that would be a concern is if an adjuster said, "This $15,000 is non-negotiable. If you don't accept it within ten days, it will be withdrawn." Most adjusters will not high-pressure you this way. They want you to settle without a lawyer. A non-negotiable, time-limit counteroffer may force a few cowards to settle, but it will drive most people to a lawyer to fight it out. Most of the time, an adjuster's counteroffer, especially his first one, is negotiable. But there's only one way to find out. Which of these three responses would you pick?

1. "Is $15,000 your maximum authority?"
2. "Are you negotiable, if I come down from the $50,000?"
3. "I'll split it with you and settle for $32,500."

Response number three is the worst. You have done more than give up $17,500 of negotiating power. You have also permanently eliminated the possibility of ever getting anything from your own uninsured motorist coverage, unless you go all the way to a jury trial. You have committed yourself to a figure of $32,500 without knowing how much your case is worth. There will be a time for this type of negotiating tactic. You can utilize this approach once you've determined that your case has a settlement value of $20,000–$25,000, and you have decided you are going to settle on your own. Even then, you shouldn't come down so far, so fast. An initial reduction to $45,000 would be more appropriate. Save the "split it with you" tactic until you and the adjuster are very close; perhaps $5,000–$10,000 apart. We'll discuss this in more detail later, when we reach our final settlement.

Response number two is good. You haven't actually committed yourself to a figure below the $50,000. You're forcing the adjuster to confirm that he has more money to offer, that he is negotiable. The main drawback to this response is the clear implication that you also are negotiable, that you will accept less than the $50,000. This is what you have given up in order to get something in return. But is there a way to get something for nothing?

This brings us to response number one—the ideal answer to a first counteroffer. You ask the adjuster: "Is $15,000 your maximum authority?" You are actually asking him to bid against himself. You are using the same tactics against him that he unsuccessfully tried to use against you. You're not committing yourself to a figure lower than $50,000; in fact, you're not even implying that you would accept less than $50,000. What you are doing is getting some valuable, *free* information. No matter what the adjuster says, you are getting something for nothing.

Will adjusters lie when answering the question about their maximum authority? Will they lie to seal a settlement? In my experience, most adjusters, like most lawyers, are basically honest. But lawyers and adjusters will state the facts in a light most favorable to their case.

Most likely, the adjuster will say something like, "No, that's not my maximum authority. But you'll have to get into my ballpark if we're going to settle this claim." The term ballpark is a favorite with adjusters. It refers to the range of a case's settlement value. He's telling you that he's got more money, but he wants you to come down a lot before he gives it to you. In this case you can assume that his ballpark is somewhere between $20,000 to $30,000.

What do you do next? The ball is back in your court. He's telling you that you're not going to get any more out of him unless, and until, you come down from the $50,000. But you still don't know what your case is worth. Which of these three responses will you choose?

1. "I still believe my case is worth more than $50,000. But I know to get it I'd have to get a lawyer and go to court. I'd be willing to take $45,000 now for a quick settlement."
2. "I need some time to think about it. Meanwhile, send me a letter with your $15,000 offer."
3. "Let's stop playing games. Just give me your maximum authority, and I'll say yes or no."

Response number one is still premature. You aren't sure yet what your case is really worth. You only want to come down to $45,000 when you're convinced your case is only worth somewhere in the 20s. Until then, don't come down. Remember, you can always come down a lot easier than you can go up.

I like response number three best, although it won't work on most adjusters. This is a final attempt on your part to get something for nothing, to force the adjuster to bid against himself. However, the adjuster has already told you that "you'll have to get into my ballpark" to settle the claim. Most adjusters will be unwilling to give you everything they've got, without at least getting you to reduce your demand. But you haven't really lost anything or committed yourself to anything. Once in a while, you'll get an inexperienced or overanxious adjuster who will say, "You've worn me down. Okay, my maximum authority is $20,000—not a penny more. If you want it, we can settle right now." More likely, he will say, "I already said you have got to get into my ballpark. Right now, we're just too far apart." Either way, that brings us to response number two.

We used response number three first, just to take one last shot at squeezing out some more money without giving up anything. But response number two is crucial for ending this negotiating session. First of all, you *always* want to get written confirmation of any counteroffer. You should also send the following confirming letter, just in case the adjuster neglected to send you his confirming letter. This sample letter assumes your adjuster only offered you $15,000; if you were lucky enough to get the $20,000 offer, just change the amount.

SAMPLE LETTER TO CONFIRM FIRST SETTLEMENT OFFER

Your Address and Phone Today's Date

Re: Date of Accident
Claim # 7777

Dear Adjuster:

This will confirm our conversation today, wherein you offered $15,000 to settle my claim. I will contact you with my response in the near future.

Thank you for your cooperation.

Sincerely,

When you tell the adjuster you have to think about it, he'll probably say, "No problem, take your time." In the unlikely event he gives you a time limit and says you must accept by that date, be sure to include this condition in your confirming letter.

Now, you have got at least $15,000 securely in your back pocket. It's time for another trip to those two lawyers you liked the most, back when your case had just begun. The next chapter will help ensure you keep that back pocket tightly buttoned.

INITIAL SETTLEMENT SAMPLE DEMAND LETTER

Your Address and Phone — Today's Date

Re: Date of Accident
Claim # 7777

Dear Adjuster:

Enclosed are the following:

1. Bills, totaling $2,200, and reports from Dr. Ortho, my orthopedic surgeon, including his final report indicating a 10 percent permanent impairment to the body as a whole. Please note that his 10 percent impairment rating is from an orthopedic standpoint. He specifically defers any impairment regarding carpal tunnel syndrome to the neurologist. Also, please note his discussion of the bulging discs in my neck and back, which were shown on the MRI scans. In his opinion, these bulges are the direct result of the accident, since I had no previous problems, treatment, or injuries in either area. My car insurance paid for 80 percent of his bills. However, he is still owed $440. My group insurance applied his balance toward my $500 deductible.

2. Bills, totaling $2,300, and reports from Dr. Neuro, my neurologist. He assigns a 15 percent permanent impairment to the body as a whole from a neurological standpoint. I am also enclosing a copy of his EMG report regarding the bilateral carpal tunnel syndrome. He states that the carpal tunnel syndrome is a direct result of this accident. I continue to have tingling and numbness in both hands. Dr. Neuro says it is not bad

enough to do surgery now, but I could need an operation if it continues to worsen. As you know, your own Dr. Radi confirmed the carpal tunnel diagnosis and completely agreed with Dr. Neuro's opinion. Dr. Neuro is still owed $60. My car insurance paid 80 percent of his bill. My group insurance paid him $400 after applying $60 of his balance to satisfy the deductible.

3. Bills, totaling $2,900, from Dr. Chiro, my chiropractor. He has assigned a 20 percent permanent impairment to my body. Please note numerous positive test findings. Also, he states that I will need to continue to see him for treatment on an as needed basis. Dr. Chiro was paid 80 percent by PIP; however, his 20 percent balance of $580 remains outstanding because my group insurance does not cover chiropractors.

4. Bills, totaling $3,500, and reports from the MRI Center for the scans of my knees, back, and neck. The radiologist confirms the bulging discs in my neck and back, which Dr. Ortho has discussed. The MRI Center bill has been paid in full between my car insurance and group insurance.

5. Bills, totaling $400, and records from the Goodtown Hospital Emergency Room.

6. Prescription bills for muscle relaxers, pain medications, and sleeping pills, totaling $200. These bills and the hospital bill were paid in full by the two insurance companies.

7. A subrogation lien letter from my group carrier. This indicates a total of $1,220 which my carrier paid toward my medical bills, and which it wants reimbursed out of my recovery. Also, I still owe $1,080 in outstanding bills: $580 to Dr. Chiro, $60 to Dr. Neuro, and $440 to Dr. Ortho.

8. Lost wage verification from my County School Board. This shows that my average weekly wage at the time of the accident was $500. I lost two weeks from work after the accident.

9. Pictures of my damaged car. As you can see, this was a severe impact, resulting in substantial damage. You have already paid the repair bill of $3,900.

In summary, my medical bills to date total $11,500, and my lost wages are $1,000. I will require future chiropractic treatment. I may need surgery to relieve my carpal tunnel syndrome.

My life has been seriously affected by this accident. I have always enjoyed wonderful health. I've never had any injuries or previous accidents. I used to enjoy picking up my three-year-old boy and swinging him around. I can hardly play with him at all now. I have given up my aerobics class three nights a week. I used to enjoy playing singles matches for my club team on weekends. Now, I'm just playing some social doubles, and even that is very painful. My hands hurt terribly after gripping the racket for just a little while.

In fact, picking up and holding normal household objects is difficult. My fingers are always tingling. This keeps me up at night. My body is aching by the end of the school day. I have become irritable with my students and my family. My marital relationship has been adversely affected. And it seems like my problems, especially the carpal tunnel syndrome, are getting worse instead of better. I'm faced with the likelihood of gradual deterioration until I'm forced to have surgery. This is all due to the negligence of your insured, who was clearly at fault. I was stopped at the red light when he rear-ended me.

Based on the above, I hereby demand the policy limits of $50,000. Please respond within thirty days from receipt of this certified letter; otherwise, I will be forced to hire a lawyer to file a lawsuit.

Sincerely,

Checklist IV (Rules of Negotiating)

1. Policy limit demand (start at the top).
2. Include specifics on how injury has affected your life.
3. Specify time limit to respond.
4. Never give up something without getting something in return.
5. Try to get something for nothing.
6. Read between the lines. What is implied? What isn't said?
7. Get counteroffer.
8. Confirm counteroffer in writing.

CHAPTER 8

How to Use Lawyers and Doctors Instead of Being Used by Them

Most people assume that all lawyers have a standard personal injury contingency fee, just as there is supposed to be a standard real estate contract, or a standard percentage of the estate for probate fees. It is true that there are general guidelines, and that many lawyers try to go by these guidelines. Some states have maximum contingent fee schedules. This just means that a lawyer cannot charge *more* than a specific fee or percentage of recovery in a given situation.

For example, Florida law limits attorneys to a maximum of $33^1/_3$ percent of the total recovery before a lawsuit, or before the defense attorney has filed an Answer, if there is a lawsuit. Once the defense attorney files the Answer, it is considered to be at issue, which means a trial date can be requested. Under Florida law, as soon as the Answer is filed, the lawyer's maximum fee can go up to 40 percent, even if the case is settled the next day. Other states may have different maximum fee schedules.

Nothing, however, prohibits a lawyer from charging *less* than the maximum. And nothing prohibits you from trying to negotiate the best deal you can, if you decide you need a lawyer's services. Not everything in life is negotiable. Not every lawyer will be willing to reduce his standard fee, but you lose nothing by trying.

Right now, you've got a decision to make. You can finish negotiating your own case, and take whatever you can get over $15,000 without a lawsuit. Or, you can hire a lawyer in the hope that he can get you more. But what if you hire a lawyer, and you end up with less because of his fee and extra legal costs?

Remember, I said you have that $15,000 in your tightly buttoned back pocket. You've been negotiating with the adjuster. Now you get to negotiate with your prospective lawyer. Your goals are: 1) Don't lose the $15,000; 2) Find out how much your case is worth; 3) Decide if it's worth the risk of filing a lawsuit.

If you are going to file a lawsuit, you must have a lawyer representing you. We're not talking about small claims court here. This is the big time. To make an informed decision on whether to file suit, you have to know how much your case is worth. To get that information, you have to go to a lawyer who specializes in personal injury cases. But what's to prevent him from recommending a lawsuit, or giving you an inflated value, just to get your case? That's where goal number one comes in; don't lose the $15,000.

If you followed my advice, you consulted with several lawyers right after your accident. You took extensive notes on what they said. You met personally with a few of them. Hopefully, at least two made a favorable impression. Whom did you trust the most? Who made you feel comfortable? Who seemed the most knowledgeable and experienced? Who answered your questions most clearly and directly? Who returned your phone call within a reasonable time? Who spent the most time with you? Who seemed to really care about you? All of these questions are part of the criteria you should consider when choosing your two finalists.

Find out if your state has a special program for certifying lawyers in certain specialties. Some states may only require that a lawyer, to call himself a specialist, be practicing for a certain number of years and take a certain number of hours of continuing legal education credit. If so, you can have a personal injury lawyer "specialist" who has never handled a jury trial in his life. There are states, however, that require a lawyer to handle a certain number of jury trials in his career and also to pass a special test in order to become certified. In those states, certification should certainly be a major factor in your choice.

If you can't narrow it down, make appointments with three or four you liked, as long as you confirm that this second consultation is still free. The lawyer may want to speak to you on the phone first. He's probably forgotten about you in the eight months since the first meeting. Just remind him that you met with him, you liked him, you don't have a lawyer yet, and you have been offered $15,000. That should catch his interest enough to offer you a second free consultation.

When you see him, bring your entire file. This should include all the correspondence, especially your demand letter asking for the $50,000 and the counteroffer of $15,000. Bring all the hospital and medical bills, records and reports. Include the following: tax returns, verification of lost wages, your car insurance and medical insurance policies, the police report, ambulance report, pictures of your car damage, bills for car repair and car rental, cancelled checks for house cleaning services, witness statements, payout sheet showing what your insurance has covered, round-trip mileage for every doctor, your diary, and a summary of how the accident has affected your life.

Let him review everything. Answer his questions directly and truthfully. Eventually, you'll be talking about your $50,000 policy limit demand and their $15,000 counteroffer. Ask him how much the case is worth. Can you sue your own company for uninsured motorist coverage? Does stacking apply? (Remember stacking from chapter 2? That's where you can add together the $50,000 uninsured motorist coverage on your car and your husband's car, which means you could get up to $100,000 over and above the other driver's $50,000.)

Ask him if he would file a lawsuit if he takes the case. Have him explain the risks of going to court. These vary in every state. Is mediation required before the case can go to trial? A mediator, unlike an arbitrator, generally has no power to make a decision. His job is to help the plaintiff and defendant reach a fair settlement instead of putting it in the hands of a jury. Ask the lawyer what percentage of cases settle at mediation. What does he think the chances are that your case will go all the way to a jury trial? How long will the process take? Finally, if you haven't already discussed it, ask him about his fee. Here are three ways to bring up the subject. Which do you prefer?

1. "If you take my case, how will you work your fee?"
2. "I'll give you 40 percent of whatever we get over $15,000; the first $15,000 is mine."
3. "I'm still not sure if I want a lawyer, but if I decide I do, how much will you charge me?"

With number two, you're making the lawyer an offer without giving him a chance to make one first. You are violating the primary rule of negotiating: Don't give up something for nothing—do try to get something for nothing. Your general tactic in number two is fine, but save it for later on. Who knows? Perhaps, if you give him the chance, and he wants your case badly enough, the lawyer will make you a better offer. Why offer him 40 percent over $15,000 if he might take less?

Numbers one and three both ask for the same thing: an offer from the lawyer of how much he's going to charge. However, number three, although honest, may get some lawyers angry. After all, this is already your second consultation with him. He's probably invested about two hours in your case with nothing to show for it. You're already not on his favorite persons list. You're going to get him even more annoyed if you tell him, in effect, that you're still shopping around. If he's angry and annoyed, he's not likely to offer you his best deal.

Number one does not state that you are going to hire him on the spot if you like his offer. But it also doesn't make him feel like you are going to walk out, no matter what he says. The words "if you take my case" are sweet music to his ears. The lawyer interprets them as meaning "This lady will sign if my price is right." He's motivated to make his fee attractive enough so it will be an offer you can't refuse.

Let's get back to the value of your case, because that will be a key factor in your deciding how to proceed. Generally, the value of a case before a lawsuit is filed is less than its value once litigation has begun. If a plaintiff's lawyer does a good job taking depositions and preparing the case, he should be able to persuade the defense attorney that it's worth more money. This is particularly true if the prelitigation offer was unreasonably low.

The defense attorney will want several months to take his depositions, do his discovery work, and make his fee by billing the insurance company at an hourly rate. If your case is strong, he's not going to want to go to a jury trial just to have a big verdict entered against his client. He will put in a reasonable number of hours to learn about your case and to help him pay his bills. Then, the defense attorney will recommend that the insurance company make a higher offer.

So, when you discuss the value of your case with the lawyer, talk about prelitigation and postlitigation values. For example, he may say, "They've offered you $15,000. That's very low for your case. Without a lawsuit, we should be able to get between $20,000 and $25,000. If we file suit, we shouldn't consider less than $30,000, and we'll try for $40,000."

You ask, "Does that mean we can't get more than the $50,000 policy limit?" The lawyer responds, "The only way we can get more than the $50,000 and go after your uninsured motorist coverage is if you have the hand surgery for your carpal tunnel syndrome. Then we might have a case worth $50,000–$100,000."

This is the first time a lawyer has been so specific in telling you how much more your case is worth with surgery. He's right. Why does having surgery make such a difference? If the surgery is successful, it should alleviate your pain and make you feel better. If you have less pain and suffering, shouldn't your case be worth less?

That's not the way most juries think. Pain and suffering is an abstract concept. A juror can't feel your pain. In most cases, a juror is skeptical as to whether you're really hurt at all. If your doctor is recommending surgery, that still doesn't mean much, because the doctor for the insurance company will say you definitely don't need surgery. It's just one doctor's opinion versus another, and it's all hypothetical.

But if you actually had to "go under the knife," most jurors would realize that you did have a serious injury. You can't fake surgery. In addition, you'll have many more hospital and doctor bills, some of which may not be paid by insurance. That means you'll have a lot more out-of-pocket expenses as part of your claim, plus additional lost wages.

I always explain to my clients how surgery affects the value of a case. But I also tell them: "You have to do what's best for your health and your life. If you decide to have surgery, do it because you believe it will improve the quality of your life, not because it will help the case."

Incidentally, the same principle holds true for staying out of work. Some clients ask me, "Is it better for the case if I stay out of work?"

I respond, "You know your body and how work affects it. Listen to the doctor's advice, but you must make the final decision based on what is best for you. You have bills to pay and responsibilities to meet. Don't work your life around the case."

The same principle applies for surgery. Some surgeons have a reputation for being quick to recommend surgery. Some lawyers refer their clients to these doctors, hoping to make the case worth more. But this is your body we're talking about. Don't let a lawyer or doctor make the decision for you. If surgery is a serious consideration, be sure to get at least one or two independent opinions. As a general rule, elective surgery should only be considered when physical therapy and other conservative treatment have failed. When you have tried everything else and you're still in constant pain that affects your whole life, maybe you're a candidate for surgery. But you still should be calling the shots. You choose the surgeon; you decide when it will be most convenient for you.

Let's get back to you in the lawyer's office. He's just told you that, in his opinion, your case is worth $20,000 to $25,000 without suit, $30,000 to $40,000 with suit, or $50,000 to $100,000 with surgery. Have you already made your decision on surgery? We cannot go any further until you do. Do you believe there is a definite possibility that you may have surgery in the near future? If so, any good lawyer will recommend not doing *anything* further until after you have the surgery. Obviously, with the different values of your case, you can see why. So, as long as you have plenty of time before that statute of limitations runs out, hold off further negotiations or a lawsuit until after the surgery.

But, let's assume that you have decided that you definitely do not want surgery, under any circumstances. Now you've got a difficult decision to make. The lawyer has told you that without surgery your case is worth $20,000 to $25,000 without suit, or $30,000 to $40,000 with suit. Remember, in your negotiations with the adjuster he offered $15,000, but he implied he had more if you "got into his ballpark." So you have to figure that you can get at least $20,000 on your own, without the help of the lawyer. Now you have to pull out your calculator, or at least the old-fashioned pencil and paper. You have some fast figuring to do.

What did the lawyer say when you asked him, "If you take my case, how will you work your fee?" How he sets up his fee will be a big factor in your decision whether to hire him. Remember, you don't want to lose your first $15,000, and you figure you can probably get at least $20,000 on your own.

Let's assume the lawyer says, "Well, my normal fee is 33⅓ percent without a lawsuit, or 40 percent once a suit is filed. But, since you have already been offered $15,000 on your own, I'll reduce my fee to 30 percent without suit, or 35 percent after suit is filed. That should help compensate you for their first offer.

You don't need your calculator to realize that makes no sense. If he ends up settling your case without suit for $25,000, he'll take $7,500, leaving you with $17,500 (assuming he hasn't incurred any prelitigation costs, which could further reduce your net). So, since you figure you can get $20,000 on your own, you've just lost $2,500 even though the lawyer feels he's done a good job for you. No, he's going to have to work harder and do better than that.

Lay it on the line for him. Tell him, "Look, I feel I earned the first $15,000. I'd only consider hiring you if you take a contingency over that. The first $15,000 is mine, no matter what we get, or how we get it."

He might say, "Okay, I'll take 50 percent of anything over $15,000, with or without suit. Of course, any costs I advance will also come out of it."

Not bad. At least you've kept your pocket buttoned on the first $15,000. But, if you accept these terms, you would have to get over $25,000 just to net $20,000. Lay these figures out for the lawyer and ask him, "Can't you do any better than that?"

At this point, he might say, "I think I can do better for you than you can do on your own. I've got an excellent reputation in the legal community and with the insurance companies. I've sued this insurance company several times and gotten some big verdicts. They're going to pay out a lot more on your claim because I'm representing you. If we file suit, I'll be doing a lot of additional work, and I'll be earning every penny of that 50 percent over $15,000. But I'll tell you what I'll do; if we settle without suit, I'll go 40 percent over the first $15,000. But that's it—that's my final offer. If you're interested, we can sign the papers now, and I'll get right to work. If not, I wish you well."

Whatever you decide at this point, you're going to come out a winner. If you hire the lawyer, and he ends up getting $30,000 without suit, his fee will only be $6,000 instead of $9,000 to $12,000. If you decide to settle on your own, you should get at least $20,000–$25,000. Maybe you will be lucky and win a little more. You decide you don't want to get involved in the time, effort, and risks of a lawsuit. And, since it looks like you can do just as well without a lawyer at this point, you decide to go all the way and settle on your own.

You walk out of the lawyer's office knowing that your case is worth $20,000 to $25,000, without suit, and without surgery. Now you're ready for the best part—final negotiations and settlement. The moment of truth has arrived.

CHAPTER 9

Settling Your Case for Top Dollar

Give the adjuster a call. Say something like, "I've consulted with a few lawyers. They all want my case, and they feel I can get a lot more if I go to court. But I wanted to give it one last shot to try to settle on my own. I'll come down to $45,000. If you really want to settle without lawyers and lawsuits, you'll offer me your maximum authority."

The adjuster will probably say, "I can't give you $45,000, or anywhere near that. If you want to shoot the dice and go to court, good luck. But the lawyer's fees and costs will eat up whatever higher amount you might get. My maximum authority is $20,000. We can settle right now for that amount. I'll send you the release and check, in today's mail."

What's your next step? Choose from these responses:

1. "I'll take it. Send the check."
2. "My bottom line is $25,000. Get me that and we've got a deal; otherwise, I'll hire a lawyer and go for the $50,000 policy limit."

3. "We're $22,500 apart. I'll split the difference with you and settle for $31,250."
4. "You came up $5,000. I'll come down $5,000 to $40,000. Since $20,000 is your maximum authority, please convey my reduced demand of $40,000, and try to get additional authority. I won't hire a lawyer while we're still negotiating. How long before you think you can get back to me?"

Did you choose number four? Great! You're learning fast. If you chose number one, go back to page one of this book. Number two leaves you no room at all to negotiate—you've backed yourself into a hopeless corner. You're still too far apart for the "split the difference" tactic of number three.

With number four, you still have plenty of room to negotiate. You're talking on the adjuster's wave-length. You're accepting the fact that his maximum authority is $20,000, but that authority was given to him back when you demanded the $50,000 policy limits. Even if he is lying about his maximum authority, you are giving him the opportunity to redeem himself. The circumstances have sufficiently changed for him to request additional authority. The worst that can happen is that he'll come back to you and say he's firm on the $20,000. You're not going to lose the $20,000. More likely, he will get some additional authority. Your next round of negotiations will be aimed at bringing you close enough so that he'll be forced to offer his new maximum authority. But you'll want to still remain sufficiently apart to force him to go back one last time.

Be sure you confirm in writing the highlights of your negotiations with a letter like this:

SAMPLE LETTER TO CONFIRM NEW SETTLEMENT OFFER

Your Address and Phone — Today's Date

Re: Date of Accident
Claim # 7777

Dear Adjuster:

This will confirm our conversation today. I reduced my demand from the $50,000 policy limits to $45,000. You offered me $20,000, which you advised was your maximum authority.

I then reduced my demand to $40,000 and asked you to request additional authority. I stated that I won't hire a lawyer while we're still negotiating.

I look forward to your response in the near future.

Sincerely,

Now you just have to wait for his next phone call. You're almost home free. The worst that can happen is that he will tell you he could not get any additional authority, in which case you can still accept the $20,000. Remember, you're never going to lose their last offer, unless the adjuster specifically states that the offer has a time limit and is not negotiable. Such high pressure tactics are rare. The adjuster risks forcing you to hire a lawyer, which is exactly what he doesn't want you to do.

More likely, the adjuster will call you back within a week or two, and begin with something like,

"I've got good news for you. I really had to fight to get additional authority, but I finally got it. We can settle your case for $22,500. Believe me, that's a lot more than you'd get a couple of years from now if you hire a lawyer and have to pay all his costs and fees. I can send you the release today; or even better, I can come over and give you the check immediately when you sign the release, and I notarize it. Do we have a deal?"

Remember what I said earlier about reading between the lines of the adjuster's statements. Everything he says is important, but also what he doesn't say can be significant. Ask yourself these questions: Is $22,500 his absolute maximum authority? Is it negotiable? Will I lose it if I ask for more?

Let's analyze his language. He says he received additional authority. Then he says, "We can settle your case for $22,500." He *doesn't* say "My maximum authority is $22,500." He *doesn't* say "My final offer is $22,500. If you don't take it, you'll have to hire a lawyer." He *doesn't* say "This is not negotiable." Reading between the lines, you can tell that he must now have more authority than the $22,500, but he's hoping to talk you into settling for less than his maximum.

Assuming that we've correctly analyzed his position, how would you answer?

1. "Come on now. Stop beating around the bush. Give me your new maximum authority, and I'll tell you whether we can settle."
2. "You came up $2,500. I'll come down $2,500, to $37,500."
3. "Let's cut through all this. Give me $30,000, and we'll settle it right now."
4. "We're too far apart. I'm not going to reduce my demand any further unless you get into my ballpark."

Which of the above is the worst response? Is your intention to settle the case as soon as possible, for as much as possible without a lawyer? If so, then number four is the worst, since you're forcing a stalemate. The adjuster is not going to "bid against himself" and "get into your ballpark" without a good faith reduction on your part. If you stick to your $40,000, he's going to stick to his $22,500. As far as he's concerned, this is a chess game and the next move is yours.

Response number three isn't bad, but you have come down too much at once. You're almost telegraphing that you'll be happy to take $25,000. If you come down to $30,000 that fast, there's no way the adjuster will ever give you more than $25,000.

That leaves responses number one and two. You're really

getting the hang of this if you said, "Let's try number one first. If that doesn't work, we'll use number two." Number one is another attempt by you to get something for nothing. A smart adjuster will respond, "Tell me your bottom line and I'll tell you whether we can settle." He's pulling on you what you tried to pull on him. But an inexperienced adjuster may just fall for it and say, "Okay. I've got $25,000. That is my maximum authority. Not a penny more."

If the adjuster won't fall for your trap, then number two is a perfectly valid negotiating technique; come down the same amount that he comes up. If that's the pace he's setting, you're comfortable with it. What you are saying is: where you lead, I'll follow. If you make a bigger move, then I will, too. You also haven't tipped your hand, so the adjuster remains unsure of your true bottom line.

If, in fact, the adjuster does have only $25,000 in authority, he's likely to offer it at this point. If he's got a little more, he's still likely to offer $25,000, to see if you'll go for it.

Let's assume the adjuster says, "I'll give you $25,000, but that's as far as I can go at this point. Do we have a settlement or not?" Which of these responses would be suitable?

1. "Let's split the difference and settle for $31,250."
2. "I'll come down to $35,000."
3. "Let me think about it. I'll send you a letter."

If you answered number one or two, you made a big mistake; you didn't listen to the adjuster's words. In particular, you missed one little phrase: "at this point." The adjuster specifically told you that he would not make *any* additional offers during this conversation. Therefore, any reduction in your demand "at this point" would be like bidding against yourself. He has left you only two options: accept the $25,000 (I didn't even include that response, because I know you're smarter than that by now), or end the conversation with response number three. So, here's the letter you send now.

SAMPLE LETTER CONFIRMING OFFER AND MAKING COUNTEROFFER

Your Address and Phone Today's Date

Re: Date of Accident
Claim # 7777

Dear Adjuster:

This will confirm our most recent conversation. You increased your offer to $22,500. I reduced my demand to $37,500. You then offered $25,000 and stated you could not go any further at that point.

I have given this a lot of thought. Since we are so close, it would be a shame to let our negotiations fall apart, forcing me to retain a lawyer. But I don't want to accept $25,000. However, I would be willing to accept $34,000.

Again, I will not hire a lawyer if there is still hope we can settle. I look forward to hearing from you. Thank you for negotiating with me in good faith.

Sincerely,

Does this letter puzzle you? What difference does it make if you reduce the demand in the letter or on the phone? And why pick $34,000 as the figure? If he was setting the pace with an increase of $2,500, why should you jump down $3,500?

Let's first discuss the strategy of making your next counteroffer by letter. As a general rule, a written offer or demand is stronger than one given over the phone. The offer is in black and white. It is clear. It is specific. It is powerful. In this case, you also have allowed a few days to go by. The adjuster's frame of mind—that he could not go any further at that point—is lost in the past.

He has negotiated on many other claims since then. When he gets your letter, with a new, lower counteroffer, he'll be starting out fresh. If $25,000 was his maximum, he'll be open to seeking additional authority from his supervisor, on the basis of your reduced, written counteroffer. He's got something tangible to show his supervisor, not just a phone message from you. The language of your letter is conducive to further negotiations. You're only $9,000 apart, having narrowed the gap enormously from the original $50,000 demand and $15,000 counteroffer. The adjuster and his company are not going to let you off the hook and allow some trial lawyer to snare you. They will, very likely, give you a little more money.

So why come down $3,500, instead of $2,500? This indicates that you're willing to set the pace. By doing so, you're inviting the other side to join you. Even if they don't come up $3,500, they're likely to increase their offer at least $1,000–$2,500, just to show good faith. At this point, you have to figure that anything over $25,000 is gravy. Remember when you had your consultation with the lawyer in our last chapter, you figured you could get $20,000 to $25,000 on your own. You're getting close to your payoff, which will make all your time and effort (and reading this book) worthwhile.

Ten days later, you get the following letter from the adjuster.

SAMPLE LETTER FROM ADJUSTER

Date

Dear Claimant:

I acknowledge your letter of February 25, 1994 to settle for $34,000. As you know, my maximum authority was $25,000. I have reviewed your file one more time with my supervisor. Frankly, he wasn't thrilled to see me again. Finally, I persuaded him to give me a little more in a final effort to settle. He has authorized me to offer you $26,500.

I am enclosing a release for that amount. Please sign it, with your husband, in the presence of two witnesses and a notary. Upon receipt of the executed release, I will promptly forward you your check.

Sincerely,
Adjuster

Congratulations. You're already into gravy territory. But we're not quite finished yet. Let's analyze the adjuster's letter. First of all, the sending of a release is a common tactic successfully used by many insurance companies. The release seems to imply a firm and final offer. But the implication is an illusion. The release is nothing more than a standard form used by the insurance company to settle every case. If you don't sign it, you haven't lost anything. If you end up agreeing on a higher figure, it will take the adjuster two minutes to send out a new release.

Now, let's analyze the contents of his letter. Does he say this is his *final* offer? No. Does he say this is his maximum authority? No. Does he give you a time limit on accepting the $26,500? No. What he does say is that his supervisor "has authorized me to offer you $26,500." Reading between the lines, you realize he is saying that he has obtained additional authority from his supervisor and he would like you to settle for $26,500. You can infer that he's got a little more.

Give him a call. We'll do a confirming letter after your conversation. What do you say?

1. "Are you firm on $26,500, or do you have a little more room if I come down some more?"
2. "Let's settle it right now. Give me $28,000 and we've got a deal."
3. "We're $7,500 apart. I'll split it with you. I can settle for $30,250."

If you answered number two, you've still got a lot to learn. Why come down so much? You know he won't give you exactly what you ask for. The best you can hope to do is get him up to $27,000 or $27,500, and then you have no more room to negotiate.

If you answered number three, you're doing a little better; however, you have still come down $3,750 when they only came up $1,500—you look a little too anxious. You're giving them too much without getting enough back.

Number one is the best opening to this negotiating session.

You're using one of the rules we learned earlier: try to get something for nothing. Yes, you are implying that you're negotiable, but the adjuster already knows that. But you're not committing yourself to a figure until he tells you that he is also negotiable. At this point, he's not going to risk letting you off the hook, especially assuming he does have additional authority. So he'll probably say something like this, "You're going to have to come down a lot; otherwise, our offer is firm at $26,500."

Did you just get something for nothing? Did the adjuster answer your question? If you answered "no" to either of my questions, re-read the adjuster's response. What's the key word? The key word is not "firm." The key word is "otherwise." You did get something for nothing. The adjuster did answer your question, and a lot more directly than it appears. Remember, your question was "do you have a little more room if I come down some more?" His answer is that he is firm on $26,500 *unless* ("otherwise") you come down a lot.

Now you have to figure out what he means by "a lot." Which number should be your next move?

1. $32,000
2. $30,000
3. $29,500
4. $28,000

Response number one, $32,000, does not come down nearly enough. A reduction of $2,000, which still leaves you over $5,000 apart, is certainly not going to be considered "a lot." Response number four, $28,000, comes down too much. You've jumped from $34,000 to $28,000, leaving only $1,500 separating you and the adjuster. You already know that you'll never get exactly the amount you request; therefore, the best you could hope to do is to get the adjuster up another $500 to $1,000, for a maximum possible settlement of $27,500.

That leaves responses number two and three. What difference does it make if you say $30,000 or $29,500? It's the same difference as your local car dealer offering a sale price of $19,999 instead of $20,000. That extra dollar means nothing as a practical matter; however, psychologically, it sounds much cheaper, because it's into the teens instead of the 20s. Why did Jack Benny always stay at age thirty-nine? Why do people suddenly feel a lot older at age forty, or fifty, or sixty, than they did a day earlier?

Obviously, then, the best response in our negotiations is number three—$29,500. You have come down "a lot"—$4,500. Psychologically, you have also broken the $30,000 barrier; you are now into the 20s, the adjuster's "ballpark." I can guarantee you that you'll now get some more money from the adjuster. (Sure, it helps that I'm making this up as I go along, but my guarantee doesn't go just for the hypotheticals in this book. It's based on over twenty years of experience and successfully settling thousands of personal injury cases.)

So you say to the adjuster, "I'm going to come down a lot, because I trust you when you tell me that, if I do, you'll come up more. I'll come down $4,500 to $29,500. But I'm firm on that, unless you come up a lot."

Again, you are speaking the adjuster's special language, a language based on implications, inferences, bluffs, and counterbluffs. You have listened to the adjuster, you have come down a lot as he requested, and you have used his own style to force him to make the next move.

He pauses for a moment. Do not speak in the silence. Do not weaken your response while he searches for his. Then he says, "You're a tough negotiator. I'm not going to beat around the bush. I've got $28,000. That's our absolute top dollar. It's my maximum authority. I don't have a penny more."

Do you take it? Or do you make one final effort to squeeze out a few more dollars? You should take the offer only if you risk losing it otherwise. The adjuster didn't say, "This is not negotiable. If you don't accept within seven days it will be withdrawn." Therefore, it can't hurt to go for it, one more time. Tell him you'll think about it, and let him know soon. Then, write this letter:

SAMPLE LETTER FOR FINAL SETTLEMENT NEGOTIATIONS

Your Address and Phone Today's Date

Re: Date of Accident
Claim # 7777

Dear Adjuster:

This will confirm our most recent conversation, wherein I came down to $29,500, and you came up to $28,000. I really did not plan on settling for less than $30,000, so I'm already below my "bottom line." However, I do appreciate your willingness to negotiate with me in good faith. Therefore, I would be willing to go even lower, to $29,000, to settle this case now.

I realize that $28,000 is your maximum authority, and that you have already gone out on a limb for me by going back to your supervisor so many times. But now, we're only $1,000 apart. I respectfully request that you try one last time to get the additional $1,000 so we can finally resolve this claim.

Thank you for your patience.

Sincerely,

This letter is highly complimentary to the adjuster, which will hopefully put him in the right mood. It also forces him to return, with your letter, for that final trip to his supervisor. Only three things can happen: they will remain firm on the $28,000; they will give you $29,000, or they'll give you something in between. Which do you think it will be?

Four days later, you get this letter:

SAMPLE LETTER OF FINAL OFFER FROM ADJUSTER

Dear Claimant:

We received your letter, reducing your demand to $29,000. Enclosed is a Release for $28,500. This is not subject to further negotiation. We will treat any additional counteroffer as a rejection, and we will be forced to withdraw this offer.

I trust this will not be necessary. Please sign the release in the presence of 2 witnesses and a notary and return it to me in the enclosed envelope. You will also need to contact me regarding the subrogation lien of Teachers' Health Insurance. I must put their name on the settlement draft, or receive a release of lien from them. Please advise.

Sincerely,
Adjuster

Congratulations. This is the release which you sign and return. You have just successfully settled your own personal injury case for much more than you would have likely received with a lawyer representing you. How much did you save? Assume you hadn't read this book and just hired a lawyer right after the accident. Let's say he ended up settling your case, without suit, for $30,000, with a $10,000 fee (33⅓ percent). Even if he had no costs (which is unlikely), and the medical bills remained the same, you still saved yourself $8,500. Even if you had hired the lawyer after getting the $15,000 offer, you're probably still coming out ahead by at least $3,000–$4,000.

Now, what about that subrogation lien? That's the amount paid toward your bills by Teachers Health Insurance. The next chapter will help you deal with your own group health insurance. You're one step away from collecting your well deserved payoff.

CHAPTER 10

Settling Subrogation Liens and Tying Up Loose Ends

Now that you've settled your case, you expect to be paid in a few days. That may not be quite true. If a lien exists, it must be satisfied. A lien may arise when any other company pays some of your medical bills or lost wages. When you settle the case, that company is going to want its money back. The theory behind liens is that you should not be paid twice for the same damages.

The adjuster mentioned your Teachers Health Insurance. He also said something about a release of lien or putting the health carrier's name on the settlement check. A release of lien is an official document stating that your health insurance company has been paid in full.

In some states, you may not have to worry about certain types of liens, which may be abolished by statute or case law. It's important that you inquire about the status of health insurance liens when you have your free consultation with the lawyers. Other liens, such as Medicare, are governed by federal law. Federal statutes require that Medicare be reimbursed for any bills paid for treatment that was part of a personal injury settlement.

In your case, your car insurance paid for 80 percent of your medical bills. If you had medical payments coverage included in your policy, that would have picked up the other 20 percent, and you wouldn't have to worry now about your Teachers Health Insurance. However, since you didn't have the optional coverage with your car insurance, the doctors submitted their bills to your group health policy to pay their balances. Shortly after you started seeing the doctors, your Teachers Health Insurance began receiving claim forms from your doctors requesting payment on the 20 percent balances. You may remember that your group plan sent you a form to sign, with instructions that there would be no payments until the signed form was returned. So you signed it, and forgot about it, until now.

It's up to you to contact your group insurance. Find out who is in charge of subrogation liens. This may be a different person than the one who was responsible for paying the doctors. Phone and write your group health insurance company to request a written accounting of all bills paid in your accident case. This is called a "payout sheet." You also need to request that the company state in writing the total amount of lien they are claiming. You should also ask them to provide you with a copy of your policy, or at least that portion of the policy which entitles them to claim a lien. Ideally, you should have had this policy before you signed the letter from your company. The policy must specify that the company is entitled to be paid back if you collect the money from a third party; otherwise, you are under no obligation to voluntarily allow them this privilege.

Let's assume that such a clause does exist in your policy, since it is a fairly standard clause with most group health insurance carriers. You get a payout sheet, and a letter stating that your company has paid out $2,700 in benefits and it wants to be paid back from your settlement. Your health insurance company has also put the other driver's car insurance company on written notice. This notice tells the other driver's company that your company has a lien on your settlement. That's why the adjuster who settled your case told you he would need to put the name of

Teachers Health Insurance on the settlement check or get a release of lien from them.

You don't want Teachers Health Insurance to be put on the check for $28,500. You will then be at their mercy, and they can insist on being paid in full before they agree to endorse the check. In fact, they will probably require you to endorse the check over to them. Then you'll have to wait for them to send you a check for the difference.

The better way to handle this is to use the same negotiating tactics you have already learned in this book. Most health insurance companies are happy if they get about 2/3 of their lien paid back. When they are dealing with a plaintiff's lawyer, they frequently offer 1/3 of the total lien as compensation to the lawyer to assist them in getting the other 2/3 paid back. Some lawyers will accept this 1/3 as an extra fee on top of their already lucrative percentage of the settlement. I have never done that, since I believe it is a conflict of interest bordering on unethical behavior. In effect, I would be selling out my client to collect some extra money for myself. Our firm always takes the position that whatever reduction we obtain on the subrogation lien goes directly to the client.

Since the group health insurance company doesn't care who gets that 1/3, it will be just as willing to deal directly with you. Therefore, you should start out by asking your health insurance company to waive its lien entirely. This is analogous to asking the negligent driver's insurance company for its policy limits. Always start as high (or, in this case, as low) as you can go. While it would be rare for a company to agree, you may get the company to bid against itself. If your health insurance company comes back and says it will reduce its lien from $2,700 to $2,200, you have already obtained almost a 20 percent reduction—and $500 more in your pocket—without having given up anything.

Next, use the strategy we employed earlier; since the company reduced the lien $500, offer $500. to settle the lien in full. Remember, you are in the reverse position now. You're like the other driver's insurance company; this money is coming out of your pocket. Don't be in any rush to give your health carrier more than is absolutely necessary. Be tough. Say you've settled the case on your own, but you are willing to go to small claims court if necessary to dispute the value of the lien. Also, state that payment will be almost immediate, if you reach an agreement now.

Be sure to confirm, in writing, all negotiations with your health carrier, just as you did with the adjuster. Your $500 offer, combined with your threat of small claims court (which will require your health insurance carrier to hire local counsel, at considerable expense), should prompt a further reduction on the lien.

Let's say the carrier comes down to $1,800. The adjuster tells you this is his company's standard 1/3 reduction. Do you accept? Of course not. Remember, "standards" are made to be broken. A standard is nothing more than a guideline, a starting point, just like the standard real estate contract or standard contingency fee agreement which we talked about earlier. Now that you've got the company down to its standard 1/3, any additional reduction is extra money for you. Your health insurance company came down an additional $400, so you can come up by $400, and offer them $900.

Using these and similar tactics we have discussed, you should be able to eventually settle the lien for somewhere around $1,200 to $1,600, or roughly 45 percent to 60 percent of the total. Once you have agreed on a figure, be sure to confirm it in writing. Contact the other driver's insurance adjuster again, with a copy of your confirmation letter settling the lien.

Let's say you settled it for $1,500. Suggest to the adjuster that he prepare two settlement checks: one payable to you only for $27,000, and the other for $1,500 payable to you and Teachers Health Insurance. Usually, the adjuster will agree to this arrangement. Then you can endorse the $1,500 over to your group carrier, and ask the company to send you a letter confirming that its lien is paid in full.

If possible, see if you can also get your carrier to leave your claim open, just in case you need any future medical treatment due to your injuries from this accident. If you negotiate hard, and make future medical expenses a condition of your settlement, you will have gained some extra security for yourself.

If the adjuster's company refuses to cut separate checks, you will have to get your group insurance carrier to execute a release of lien and send it to the other company. Your group carrier may insist on getting paid the $1,500 first, although it may accept a notarized letter from you guaranteeing that you'll pay the $1,500 out of your $28,500 settlement. If your group carrier won't execute the release of lien until it receives the $1,500, you'll have to pay it from your own funds, get the release of lien, and send that release to the adjuster. Then there will be no problem in getting the entire $28,500 payable to you.

There may be a few other loose ends you need to tie up. Contact the offices of each of your treating doctors. Find out if there are any balances on your bills, since it is possible that a doctor was not paid 100 percent, even between the two insurance companies.

Sometimes, a health insurance carrier will claim that a doctor's bill is unreasonably high. For example, let's say your orthopedic surgeon's initial office visit is $400, plus $200 for X rays. Your car insurance paid its required 80 percent without question, leaving $120 outstanding. However, your group carrier decided that the "reasonable and customary" initial office visit should not exceed $250, plus $150 for X rays. Therefore it only paid for 20 percent of $400, or $80, leaving $40 still unpaid. The group carrier should have sent the doctor some type of memo with its reduced payment, and you should have received a copy. Sometimes the memo will show a code or number explaining the payment, and you'll have to find the explanation corresponding to the number.

Let's assume that both auto and health insurance companies made some of these adjustments with three of your doctors. You have copies of each explanation where reductions were made. For each case, you see that one or both insurance companies reduced the payments because the bill exceeded the "reasonable and customary charge." You contact each doctor's office and determine the following:

1. The chiropractor has a balance of $1,450 out of a total bill of $7,625.
2. The orthopedic surgeon was paid $1,100 out of $1,350 in total billing.
3. The balance for the neurologist is $375; he was paid $1,475.

You may remember that each of these doctors required you to sign a document when you first started treatment. This document stated that you would be responsible for any bill not paid by insurance. So, now you owe $1,450 + $250 + $375, or a total of $2,075. Do you politely write out a check to each doctor for the full amount? Did you say: "Of course not! I'm going to try to avoid paying the doctors anything!" If so, you're just about ready to get your diploma from my Art of Negotiating School. Now, how do you go about achieving your goal?

If you remember, back in chapter 4 when you were beginning your medical treatment, I advised you to get each doctor to agree to accept whatever the two insurance companies paid. I also told you to get this agreement in writing. Let's assume the chiropractor agreed, but the other two doctors didn't. If your chiropractor has conveniently forgotten, show him the written agreement. Okay, now you're already off the hook for his $1,450 balance.

The two specialists only agreed that they would wait to be paid any balances out of your settlement. Now they want their money. Before you pay them a penny, you can get their help in attempting to get the medical insurance companies to reconsider. Get those explanations from the insurance company for each reduced bill. Review these reductions with the two doctors. Ask each doctor to write a letter to the company explaining why the treatment and bill was reasonable and necessary. At worst, the company will still deny the bill; however, there is a chance that some additional payments will be made.

Let's assume that the orthopedic surgeon is paid an additional $50 and the neurologist an additional $75, based on their explanatory letters. That leaves a balance of $300 for the neurologist and $200 for the orthopedic surgeon. Now, use the same philosophy of negotiating you have learned in this book. Start out by asking each doctor to waive their final balances. They'll probably say that you have received an excellent settlement, and their bills were considered as part of that settlement. Also, they will remind you that you signed a lien guaranteeing them the balance out of settlement, and that they never agreed to waive anything.

You can respond by showing them the documentation that you had to pay your group carrier $1,500 out of the settlement for its lien. Most doctors won't realize this fact until you tell them. It may not result in the doctor waiving his entire balance, but it may make him more open to negotiation.

If you feel very strongly that either doctor grossly overcharged, you can diplomatically suggest that you would like to have the bill reviewed by the local medical association. Most counties have a medical association which regulates their doctors. Review boards will have regular hearings to resolve patient complaints, particularly about bills. The typical doctor does not want to waste a couple of hours of his time at a hearing to argue about $200 or $300. The mere suggestion of such a hearing may result in some doctors saying, "Okay, you win. Forget the balance."

Of course, other doctors may perceive that you are threatening them, and they might get angry or defensive. You also risk alienating this doctor arguing over a small amount, and you never know when you might need him again. That's why I suggested being diplomatic and using this approach only if you are convinced that you have been overcharged.

Regardless of which tactics you choose to use, be sure you get the doctor to at least make a counteroffer. Negotiate with the doctors just as you did with the insurance adjusters. Whatever they agree to reduce is that much more in your pocket. If you handle yourself with dignity, hopefully you will both earn the doctor's respect and not lose him as your physician if the need arises.

Congratulations again. Your case is over. You have regained your health, been fairly compensated for your pain and suffering, and learned some valuable lessons for the rest of your life. And you did it all on your own.

CHAPTER 11

Other Types of Accident Cases

There are many variations of the standard car accident case. If you are involved in one of the following types of accidents, you should still take the basic steps, and use the techniques of settlement we have already discussed. However, you should be aware of the special circumstances for each variation.

Passenger

If you are injured as a passenger, the standard car accident case becomes a little more complicated. First of all, there is the liability issue. Who caused the accident? When I discussed comparative negligence, I said your recovery would be reduced by the percentage you were at fault. Generally, a passenger is not considered to be at fault, unless he did something to the driver to cause the accident. However, in some states, you may be considered partially at fault for your injuries if you were not wearing a seat belt.

Let's assume that you are a passenger in your friend's car. You are wearing your seat belt and taking a nap. Suddenly, you are awakened by a crash. Your lip is bleeding, and your head is hurting.

You should follow the same advice discussed earlier in the standard car accident. If you go to the emergency room and your lip requires stitches, be sure to insist that a plastic surgeon does the work. Now, who is responsible for your hospital and doctor bills? And whose insurance company will pay your settlement?

In most passenger cases, there are at least three or four different insurance companies involved. You should still report the accident to your own insurance company. Remember that Personal Injury Protection (P.I.P.), which pays for your own medical bills and lost wages, follows you wherever you go. This is true unless your policy or your state's law makes specific exceptions. So your P.I.P. coverage should pay at least some of your medical bills, whether you're a driver, passenger, pedestrian, bicyclist, etc.

Filing a claim with your company should not affect your premium, since you were not at fault. However, there are no guarantees. Some insurance companies will raise your rate or even cancel your coverage if you make any kind of claim at all. Should that prevent you from making the claim? Absolutely not. That's why you are paying the premium. And if your insurer wants to cancel you for one claim, you can certainly find a better, more reliable company.

As soon as possible after the accident, get all necessary information from your friend regarding his insurance coverage. Try to obtain a copy of his policy, or at least the declaration page showing what areas are covered. Even if your friend was not at fault, his insurance may be very important and valuable to you.

The first coverage which may apply is called medical payments (med-pay). Usually, med-pay follows the car while P.I.P. follows the person. So, your P.I.P. might pay 80 percent of your bills, and your friend's med-pay would pay the other 20 percent. Depending on the policy and the state, these percentages may vary.

If you also have med-pay on your policy, the two companies might each pay half the benefits. If your friend's company is considered primary, it must pay all of its med-pay benefits before your company will pay anything. The most important thing from your standpoint is to get both companies involved. Between the two of them, you have the best chance of getting all of your bills paid.

If your friend was at least partially at fault for the accident, his liability coverage will be important. Let's assume you live in a state where there is some kind of comparative negligence law. You may end up negotiating your settlement with your friend's company, and the other driver's company. The amount you get from each may depend on how much each driver was at fault, and on how much insurance coverage exists in each policy. When you have your free lawyer consultations, try to have copies of both policies, as well as your own. The lawyers will be able to enlighten you on how the law works in your state, based on the circumstances of the accident and the coverages available.

Let's assume your friend was not at fault at all. He was stopped at a red light and was rear-ended. In this situation, you may collect settlements from three different companies. The first or primary coverage is the liability insurance of the driver who hit you. The secondary insurance is a combination of the uninsured motorist coverage of your friend's policy and your own.

Remember at the beginning of the book when we discussed the importance of uninsured motorist coverage? In this situation, the amount of your uninsured motorist limits can be crucial to obtaining the best settlement. Let's assume your injuries are serious. You end up with a permanent facial scar above your lip. Depending on your age, sex, and the severity of the scar, your case might be worth $25,000 to $100,000 or more.

Let's say the driver who hit you only has a minimal $10,000 liability policy. You should be able to get his company to offer its full $10,000 limit. But you're probably not going to be able to accept it until you get a waiver of subrogation rights from your company, and your friend's company. This means that your company and your friend's company agree to let you settle with the other driver's insurance company. Before waiving subrogation rights, most companies will do a financial investigation to be sure the other driver has no substantial assets.

Once the other driver's company offers its limits, you'll have to negotiate with your company and your friend's company. If both of you have the same amount of uninsured motorist coverage, each company will probably pay an equal amount; however, there may be specific laws in your state, or language in the policies to cover this situation. If the amounts of coverage are different, the companies may pay you pro-rata. For example, if your uninsured motorist coverage is $50,000 and your friend's coverage is $25,000, the breakdown might be: $10,000 liability limits from the other driver, $30,000 from your company, $15,000 from your friend's company.

Sound confusing? These cases can get complicated. Just remember our basic negotiating technique: ask for the policy limits on all the policies. Get counteroffers without coming down from the policy limits. Then, if you decide to hire a lawyer, at least you'll have some money in your pocket that won't be reduced by attorney's fees.

Pedestrian

The pedestrian light blinks from Don't Walk to Walk. You step off the curb and begin to cross the street. A driver turning right doesn't see you. He slams on his brakes, but his car hits you just hard enough to knock you down.

Follow the same steps as described for auto accidents. Be sure you get all important information from the driver, including insurance details. If you have your own car insurance, your Personal Injury Protection should pay for most of your bills—remember, P.I.P. follows you wherever you go. If you don't have car insurance and don't own a car, the driver's insurance will probably pay your bills, and give you a settlement.

Of course, there will always be an issue of comparative negligence. Did you fail to look for any turning cars before crossing? Were you crossing on a Walk light? Were you inside the designated crosswalk?

Be sure to get names, addresses, and phone numbers of any witnesses. If you have an independent witness to confirm that you were in the crosswalk and the Walk light was on, you will have a much stronger case.

However, even without witnesses, you should be successful

in winning a decent settlement. In most instances, the pedestrian has the right of way. Of course, there are exceptions. The driver may have a witness who says you were jaywalking, and you suddenly darted into the street, right in front of the car. Now the burden is on you to prove that the driver could have avoided hitting you, if he was exercising reasonable care.

Once you get by the issues of who was at fault, and which insurance companies are paying your bills, the pedestrian case is similar to the standard car accident case. You'll have to go after the driver's liability insurance coverage first. If neither the driver, nor the owner of his car has liability coverage, you can make the claim under your uninsured motorist coverage. If you don't own a car, but you live with a blood relative who has a car and uninsured motorist coverage, you may be able to make a claim under that policy. Be sure to go over these circumstances during your free consultation with the lawyers.

If there is no insurance from any of these sources, you'll have to be creative enough to find someone else at fault. Was the pedestrian light or traffic signal malfunctioning? If so, perhaps you have a claim against the city, county, or state. Did big bushes or a tree prevent the driver from seeing you as he was turning? In these cases, you can try to go after the owner of the property and his homeowner's policy.

However, these types of third party liability claims are usually difficult to prove. You'll probably have little success trying to settle on your own. If your injuries are serious enough, your best bet would be to hire a lawyer, especially if you're taking on the state, or one of its subdivisions.

Be sure you find out if there's a special law on suing the state. Government entities have something called sovereign immunity. This means that you can't sue your city, county or state unless there's a law that says you can. Your state's law will provide the conditions and limitations of your claim. These limitations can include a maximum amount of recovery and a maximum percentage for an attorney's contingency fee. If a lawyer charges more than the maximum, he's breaking the law. Of course, you'll negotiate with him to take the case for less.

Bicyclist

If you are riding a bicycle, you're in a similar legal position as the pedestrian. The same types of insurance coverage situations will apply. The main differences will involve any special laws in your state, county, or city that apply to bicyclists. These special laws are discussed below. Incidentally, be sure to take pictures of your bicycle damage. If your bike is seriously damaged, or totalled, you should keep it safe in its unrepaired condition.

As a pedestrian, we discussed the issue of where you were walking. If you were in the crosswalk, and you had the Walk light, you were obeying the law. Under those circumstances, especially with a favorable witness, it is unlikely that you will be charged with any comparative negligence.

As a bicyclist, most states require that you drive in the same direction as the car traffic. If you are driving against the flow, you have one strike against you. There are also laws in many parts of the country requiring bicyclists to wear helmets. If you're not wearing a helmet, you may be considered partially at fault for your injuries, especially head injuries. This is the same concept as the seat belt laws. If you're in a car, and you're not wearing a seat belt, the defense will argue that your injuries would have been much less serious with the seat belt on. Similarly, as a bicyclist, your head injuries could have been partially or totally avoided, had you worn your helmet.

Special laws may exist if you're driving your bike at night. You may be required to have a headlight on, as well as a rear light or reflector that is clearly visible in the dark. You may also be required to wear special shoes, or clothing which stands out at night.

Even if your locality does not have all of the above laws, it's an excellent idea to follow all of the rules for safe biking. First of all, you want to protect yourself as much as possible. Then, if you are injured, despite all safety precautions, you can make the best case for the car driver being totally at fault.

Motorcyclist

If you are foolish enough to drive a motorcycle, be prepared to become acquainted with many personal injury lawyers, or read this book once a year. I have handled many motorcycle cases through the years. Rarely is the motorcyclist even partially at fault. Usually, some elderly driver, in a very large car, just doesn't see the motorcycle. Most of the time, there's nothing the motorcyclist can do to prevent the accident.

In Florida and many other states, motorcycles are not considered "motor vehicles" under the legal definition. Find out how your state classifies motorcycles. Then find out what insurance coverage is available to you.

If motorcycles are exempt from your state's laws regarding no-fault insurance, you will probably not be able to purchase personal injury protection to cover your medical bills and lost wages. Therefore, be sure you have your own private, or group medical coverage, as well as a disability insurance policy if you're unable to work. And, believe me, a serious motorcycle accident can knock you out of action for a long time.

However, most states should allow you to purchase uninsured motorist coverage along with your liability insurance. Take the maximum amount of uninsured motorist coverage. If available, take an umbrella policy with uninsured motorist coverage. Driving a motorcycle, you are already unprotected on the road. Don't allow yourself to be unprotected with insurance as well.

The only good news about motorcycle claims in many states is that you may not have to worry about any no fault threshold requirement. Thresholds, such as proving a permanent injury from the accident, can often result in the injured party losing his case in court, even though he wasn't at fault.

Let's assume your state's law exempts motorcycles from the definition of motor vehicles. This probably results in the motorcycle accident being covered under what is called common law. Under common law, any person can sue another for negligence, regardless of the severity of injuries. So, even if your injuries are not serious, the defendant's insurance company is likely to want to settle without a suit. If the defendant was at fault, the insurance company knows it will have to pay something. Without a threshold, the insurance company can't win the case and get off without paying you. Adjusters are generally anxious to settle motorcycle claims as quickly as possible, especially if the motorcyclist is totally free of blame.

Of course, this doesn't mean that you should be pressured into settling quickly. Our basic rules of negotiating still apply. Don't make your initial policy limit demand until you have finished your medical treatment and received final reports from the doctors. Also, as in the bicycle accident, be sure to take pictures of the damage to the motorcycle. If you suffered abrasions and bruises, take pictures immediately, before they heal.

Be sure you obey any law relating to motorcycles. Most important, wear your helmet at all times. If the helmet was damaged during the accident, keep it that way, and avoid using it. A severely damaged helmet can be persuasive evidence of injuries.

If an adjuster takes your statement, act and dress conservatively. Dispel any stereotype of the Hell's Angels cyclist. The more you come across as a normal person, minding your own business at the time of the accident, the more likely the adjuster will sympathize with you.

Finally, good luck. As a motorcyclist on today's roads, you need it.

CHAPTER 12

Slip and Fall Cases

Everything so far has been geared toward a typical car accident. This is the most common case and the easiest to settle. It is also possible to settle your own slip and fall case under certain circumstances.

The Easy Case

You are walking in the plant section of a department store. Your eyes are perusing the shelves looking for a certain type of fertilizer for your indoor plants. Suddenly, you slip and fall due to water on the floor. You hit your right knee hard as you land. It hurts immediately. You're afraid to get up. You realize that there is a stream of water coming from large plants down the aisle. You see a store employee with a hose watering the plants. You are lying in a large puddle. Your clothes are soaked.

You yell for help to the employee who is watering the plants. He comes over and sees you lying on the floor. He says something like, "Oh, I'm sorry, I forgot to put the cones down. I'll go get the manager." While you're lying there waiting for the manager, all you can think about is the worsening pain in your knee. But you also need to realize that your injury claim has just begun.

Everything you do from this point on will be important, if

not crucial, to successfully settling your case. Be sure that you get the full name, address, and phone number of the employee who was watering the plants. He is the most important part of your case. If the store fires him for negligence, it will be even better for you, since he will be more willing to cooperate by telling the truth. Even if he remains employed, he will have to admit that he was watering the plants as part of his job. This will overcome the biggest difficulty in most slip and fall cases; namely, notice to the defendant.

Many people believe that a store is automatically liable if an injury occurs on the premises. This is simply not true. Just as you have to prove that a driver is negligent for causing an accident, you also have to prove that a store is negligent for causing, or allowing, a dangerous condition that resulted in your injury. In the typical slip and fall case, the defendant can claim lack of knowledge of the dangerous condition.

For example, you slip in a supermarket due to some liquid on the floor. There is no way to prove how long that liquid has been on the floor. An employee may testify that, five minutes earlier, he had just been up the aisle where you fell, and there was nothing on the floor. In such cases, it is impossible to prove *actual* notice to the supermarket. The best you could hope to prove is *constructive* notice, which means that the store should have known about the liquid on the floor. Perhaps the liquid looked dirty, which would be an indication that it had been on the floor longer than five minutes. Most of the time in these cases, you have a difficult and possibly losing battle.

In our sample case, however, the employee himself was the cause of the water on the floor. He failed to put out any warning signs, cones, or other indication of a slippery floor. Since the store is responsible for the negligence of its employees, you have an unusually strong slip and fall case. If any customers witnessed the fall, get their names, addresses, and phone numbers. Ideally, you should try to obtain some photographs of the puddles, and the water leading from the plants. You can ask the paramedics to take pictures if they have a camera. You can also ask the manager to take photos, although it will not be possible for you to obtain those pictures unless a lawsuit is filed. Be sure to keep your stained clothes in exactly the condition they are in following the accident. Do not wash them or change them in any way. The stains on your clothing, including any marks on your shoes, will be valuable evidence.

When the manager comes, he will probably be making an incident report for the store. If he does not appear to be making a written report, request that he do so. Be sure to get his name, address, and phone number as well. Point out to him not only the puddle of water where you fell, but also the flow of water from the plants. Repeat what the employee told you about apologizing for not putting down cones. Insist that he call for an ambulance. Do not attempt to get up. Ask him to give you whatever information he has regarding either the insurance company, or the insurance agent for the store. If he does not know this information, ask him to give you the name and number of someone who does.

Also, make it clear to him that you never saw the water on the floor, until after you fell. Explain that you were looking at the shelves shopping for fertilizer. This is important regarding the issue of whether you yourself were negligent for failing to watch where you were going. In almost every slip and fall case, the defense will try to prove that you were negligent for failing to use due care, which is defined as what a reasonable person would do under similar circumstances. If there is an open and obvious danger which any reasonable person should have seen, it is much more difficult to successfully collect for injuries from a slip and fall case.

The manager will most likely tell the employee to clean up the floor. You should loudly insist that nothing be done until the paramedics get there, because you want them to see the condition of the floor as it was when you fell. The manager is not required to listen to you, but if you are insistent enough, he probably will.

When the paramedics arrive, be sure you point out the puddle you slipped on, as well as the water coming from the plants. Make sure that they include this information in their incident report. Try to get their names, addresses, and phone numbers, since they will also become valuable witnesses for you.

Before the paramedics take you to the hospital, ask the manager if his store will be responsible for your hospital and doctor bills. He may say, "Just send me the bills, and I'll take care of them." Be sure to tell the hospital to send the bills to the store, but also obtain copies for your file.

If your knee is seriously hurt, the hospital may offer you the option of staying overnight to have additional tests done, or of being discharged and referring you to an orthopedic surgeon. If you have the choice, it is better to stay overnight. This will emphasize the severity of your injury.

Once you are discharged from the hospital, you can follow the same basic strategy described for the sample car accident case. If your knee is your only problem, it will probably only be necessary to see an orthopedic surgeon. If, however, you start having back, neck, and/or head problems, you should proceed with the same suggested trio of treating doctors as in our car accident case: orthopedic surgeon, neurologist, and chiropractor.

Let's assume that your MRI shows torn cartilage in your knee. The orthopedic surgeon recommends surgery. As previously discussed, you should never begin settlement negotiations until after you have recuperated from your surgery.

Your negotiation tactics should be exactly the same as described in chapter 7. However, you may find that the store is "self insured." In this case, an insurance adjuster will be handling the case, but the store itself will be paying any settlement out of its own pocket. Therefore, there is no policy limit which would be the starting point of your demand. You should begin by asking for 10 to 20 percent over the highest figure that any lawyer suggested in evaluating your case following your surgery. You have a strong case. Be aggressive and confident in your negotiations. This one is a winner all the way. (See Slip and Fall Demand Letter following this chapter.)

The Tough Case

Many slip and fall cases involve "premises liability." This usually consists of some type of defect on the premises: a hole in a sidewalk, a chipped edge on a step, a steep incline, poor lighting, or any other potentially dangerous problem. When we represent a client in this type of case, the first thing that we do is hire a safety expert. This expert must go out to the scene with the client and do a thorough investigation, including taking pictures, measurements, and performing any safety tests that may be appropriate (such as testing the degree of illumination in the area at approximately the same time of day or night as the incident occurred). Without such a safety expert's report, it is very difficult to prove liability and negligence against the defendant.

Therefore, if you are serious about intending to settle this type of case yourself, you will have to hire your own expert. Of course, that means it will cost you some money up front. The expert will not take your case on a contingency. He is usually either an engineer, or has enough specialized training and experience in the field to command a healthy fee. Such an expert could charge anywhere from $500 to $5,000 for an initial investigation and report, depending on how detailed and complicated it is. Getting the expert out there as quickly as possible is of utmost importance. The longer the delay, the more likely the defendant will have repaired or changed the defect. Subsequent repair of the premises is not admissible evidence. Therefore, if you and the expert do not work quickly, you could lose your case right from the beginning.

If this is sounding too complicated and expensive for you, you may wish to hire a lawyer immediately, in order to be sure that the case is properly handled. However, if a lawyer tells you that he is going to hold off hiring an expert to save you some money, get another lawyer. You could do just as poorly by yourself, without him. The expert witness is usually the key to this type of case. Without expert testimony regarding the dangerous condition on the premises, even the greatest lawyer may be fighting a losing battle.

If you want to try to do this yourself, you're going to need to find an expert fast. The best source for finding this type of expert is usually in legal journals and periodicals. Unfortunately, the lawyers have those, too. You may be able to get a copy of your state bar association journal or magazine in your local library. If you have a law school in your area, the law library will certainly have these journals. You can also try the Yellow Pages under such headings as Safety Experts, Safety Engineers, Accident Reconstruction Experts, or under the general heading of Engineers.

Be sure to review the credentials of any expert before you hire him. Get some references from lawyers for whom he has worked, as well as other clients. Try to contact a few of those clients before making your final decision.

Again, you must act quickly. If you wait longer than a week, it may be too late. Be sure that you get many pictures of the defect in the premises immediately after the accident. If the premises have been repaired before your expert gets there, he can still examine your pictures and compare them to the premises following the repairs. He would still be able to render an opinion based on the comparison, although his testimony would be much more easily questioned.

Let's assume you hire an expert. You pay him $1,000 to do his initial investigation. After you have paid him, and he has investigated the premises, he tells you that you don't have a case. Perhaps you fell because a ramp you were walking down was too steep. Your expert tells you that the ramp conforms to all building codes and regulations. It even has hand rails on both sides for additional safety. Your expert can find nothing to explain why you fell, other than your own clumsiness. What do you do now?

First of all, try to get some of your money back from him. Let's assume you agreed, before you paid him, that the $1,000 was to include a written report. Incidentally, as with any other agreement, be sure you have a written contract. Before you sign his standard contract, go over any ambiguous language. In a questionable slip and fall case, I always insist that my safety expert specify a lesser fee if he does not provide a written report.

Now that you've saved yourself a few dollars, you have to decide whether to pursue your case. You have four options:

1. Hire another expert.
2. Hire a lawyer.

3. Forget about another expert or a lawyer, and try to settle the case yourself.
4. Forget about your claim.

Let's assume that your orthopedic surgeon's initial diagnosis is a torn cartilage in your right knee. He recommends arthroscopic surgery. Which of the options above are you going to choose?

If you chose number four, go back to page one of this book. The basic philosophy of this book is don't ever give up something without first getting something in return. Why lose your entire claim, especially since you've suffered a serious injury? Certainly, your expert's negative opinion is a serious setback, however, it doesn't mean that your case is worth nothing. At this point, no one knows about your expert's opinion, except he and you. Since he's put nothing in writing, you can just wave goodbye to him permanently. Unless, and until, the adjuster tells you that the company denies liability and refuses to pay you anything, your claim is alive.

Which of the three remaining options do you choose? At this point, you'd probably be throwing good money after bad by hiring another expert. You fell on a steep ramp, which your first expert found to be safe and in compliance with all codes. It's unlikely that, in this situation, the owner of the premises will make any changes or repairs, since there was nothing wrong with the ramp.

Should you hire a lawyer? I hope you said, "I bought this book so I wouldn't have to hire a lawyer." Good for you. Remember, you can always hire a lawyer after you've received an offer. And that lawyer can always hire a different expert.

For now, just follow the steps in the previous chapter. The strongest part of your case is that you're going to need knee surgery. Hopefully, the seriousness of your injuries will result in your getting some type of settlement, even if it only covers your medical bills and a little extra for your pain and suffering. Most insurance companies are willing to settle serious injury cases for a relatively small amount without a lawsuit, even when there is almost no negligence against their insured. Just be prepared to take a lot less than if you had a case of clear liability, such as the rear-end collision we discussed in the earlier chapters.

Here is an example of a slip and fall letter you can write to the adjuster when you fall on a slippery floor.

SLIP AND FALL SAMPLE DEMAND LETTER

Your Address and Phone   Today's Date

Re: Date of Accident
Claim # 7777

Dear Adjuster:

Enclosed are the following:

1. All bills and reports of Dr. Michael Stern, my orthopedic surgeon. As you know, I tore cartilage in my right knee when I fell. Dr. Stern performed arthroscopic surgery one month after the accident. I stayed overnight at North County Hospital. Dr. Stern was also treating me for my back injury. In his final report, he assigns a 15 percent permanent impairment to the body as a whole due to the combination of back and right knee injuries. Dr. Stern is a board certified orthopedic surgeon with an excellent reputation. Dr. Stern's total bills, including surgery, are $4,550. Traveler's, my group insurance from work, paid him $3,200. His outstanding balance is $1,350.

2. Bills and reports from the MRI Center. The right knee MRI confirms the torn cartilage. The lumbar MRI shows a slightly herniated disc at L3-L4. MRI bills total $3,000. Traveler's paid $2,400, leaving an outstanding balance of $600.

3. North County Hospital bills and records. This includes my emergency room visit the day of the accident as well as the overnight stay for the surgery. The hospital bills total $2,700. Traveler's paid $2,160. The hospital is pressuring me for the $540 balance, as you can see from the enclosed collection agency letters.

4. Bills and records from Physical Therapy Associates, to whom I was referred by Dr. Stern. I received therapy for my back for about five months. I also had therapy to strengthen my knee after surgery. Therapy

bills total $6,600. My insurance paid $4,800, leaving a balance of $1,800.

5. Receipts for prescriptions totalling $570. These were muscle relaxers and pain pills. I still require these occasionally for my back. My insurance reimbursed me $456. I paid out of pocket $114.

6. Wage loss statement from my employer, Smith & Smith, P. A. Also enclosed are my last two years of tax returns. As you know, I am a legal secretary. The statement shows my average weekly wage prior to the accident was $400 per week. I missed two weeks' work immediately after the accident. I missed three weeks following the surgery. Therefore, I incurred total lost wages of $2,000. I used up my remaining two and a half weeks of sick leave time. I still have trouble with my back when I'm working. It stiffens up when I'm sitting too long. I've got to stand up and walk around frequently. This reduces my effectiveness. I'm concerned about getting fired, because it looks like I'm just goofing off.

7. Copies of all payment sheets from Traveler's and a letter dated March 22, 1995. As you can see, Traveler's is claiming a subrogation lien of $13,016.

All hospital and medical bills total $17,420. Since Traveler's has paid $13,016 there remains $4,404 outstanding or unreimbursed.

8. Enclosed are some recent pictures of the permanent scar on my knee from the surgery. Although the scar is small, it is still noticeable. I feel self-conscious if I'm wearing anything where my knee is visible.

9. Also enclosed are pictures of the accident site. These were taken two days after I fell.

As you know, I was shopping in the plant department of your store in the North County Mall. I was walking along aisle four, looking on the shelves to my left for a small house plant. Suddenly, the floor felt wet and slippery. I tried to grab on to a shelf to prevent the fall; however, I was unable to stop. My right knee hit the floor first. I felt water all over me. I looked around and noticed a stream of water coming from the large floor plants in aisle five. The enclosed pictures marked "2" and "3" were taken from the area I fell, facing toward the aisle five plants.

I felt immediate sharp pain in my right knee. I wasn't sure if I broke anything, so I didn't attempt to get up. I cried out for help. The first one who got to me was John, a store employee. John had a hose in his hand. The first thing he said to me was something like, "I'm really sorry. I was watering the plants in aisle five. I didn't realize it got wet over here."

By this time, I was really hurting. My white slacks were soaked. I haven't had them cleaned and I still have water stains on them, as you can see from the enclosed picture. I asked John to get the manager and to call 911.

The manager, James Smith, came over and took some information from me. He told John to get a mop and warning cones to put around the area while he cleaned up. He apologized to me. He said the ambulance was on the way. He gave me his card and wrote down the 800 number of the insurance company. He said they would take care of everything.

Well, now's the time to take care of everything. The wet, slippery floor was negligently caused by the store's employee. I came in for a plant, feeling healthy and great. I left in an ambulance, with torn cartilage in my knee and a bad back. I never had any previous problems with my knee, my back, or any other injuries. I've never made an accident claim.

I enjoyed playing tennis and jogging. I was the number three singles player on my A-1 tennis team at the Racquet Club. Between my knee and my back, I wasn't able to play for six months after the accident. I just started hitting the ball again last week. I felt like a beginner. I'm walking at a decent pace now for a couple of miles, but I haven't even tried to jog. Before the accident, I was running three to five miles, three times a week.

I'm forty-five years old. I will have been married to Jim for twenty years this June. The accident has seriously affected our normal life. I was in too much pain to have marital relations at all for several weeks after the accident and several weeks after surgery.

When we have had sex, I'm not as physical or energetic as I was before the accident. My back tends to hurt during and after sex. In addition, we used to enjoy bike riding and water-skiing together. Both of these activities are too painful now. Jim is supportive and understanding, but we're just not as happy and together as we used to be.

I have consulted several lawyers. They all tell me that I can get more than the $250,000 insurance policy limits if I sue. However, I am willing to settle at this point for the $250,000 policy limits.

If we are unable to settle within thirty days, I will be forced to hire a lawyer to file suit. Naturally, we'll be going after more than $250,000. I hope that won't be necessary. I look forward to hearing from you.

Sincerely,

CHAPTER 13

Dog Bites

If you're going to get bitten by a dog, be sure the owner carries homeowner's insurance. Most homeowner policies cover damages caused by the owner's pet, even if the injury does not occur at the home. In many states, an owner is strictly liable for injuries caused by his pet. This means that you don't have to prove anything except that your injuries were caused by the owner's dog.

In some states, the owner can claim as a defense that you provoked the dog. It's not a good idea to provoke dogs, regardless of where you live. So we'll assume that you were not responsible for the dog biting you.

If the dog had his regular shots, rabies is not a problem. Rabies shots are given once a year or once every three years. Almost all homeowners are fairly current in keeping up with the shots required by their county or state. However, even if the dog does not have current shots, rabies is rarely a problem. You are okay as long as you are dealing with a known dog, which is a dog that is known to be healthy. If you are bitten by a wild or stray dog, you will have to have a series of rabies shots. Unfortunately, you will not have a case, since you will not know the owner of the dog.

Most dog bites require medical attention. Just like the car accident case, you should go to the emergency room immediately. In general, bite wounds are irrigated with an antiseptic solution. Stitches are usually not used, since the wound is likely to have substantial bacteria. Stitching the wound would result in sealing in the unwanted bacteria. You will be given a tetanus shot if you have not had one within a few years. The emergency room doctor may also prescribe antibiotics to prevent bacterial infection.

If possible, get someone to take pictures of your wound. Try to obtain the details of the homeowner's insurance. Call the company as soon as possible. The coverage may include separate payment for medical bills, similar to premises insurance in slip and fall cases. If so, submit your initial hospital and doctor bills right away, along with duplicates of the pictures.

The key elements in evaluating a dog bite case are whether there will be a permanent scar and, if so, where the scar is located. Most likely, the scar will be permanent. A plastic surgeon will usually say that, if you still have a scar after six months, it is permanent.

Make an appointment with a plastic surgeon as soon as possible after the bite. He should re-examine you approximately six months after the injury. Request that he prepare a narrative report specifying that the scar is permanent and have him include a discussion of any cosmetic surgery that would improve the appearance of the scar. The discussion should include approximate surgical fees and other fees, such as hospital and anesthesia. Tell the doctor you will pay his normal fee for this narrative report, since this is a charge not paid by medical insurance. You will be sending in this report with your policy limit demand letter. (See Dog Bite Sample Demand Letter following this chapter.)

The plastic surgeon may take additional pictures of the scar at the six-month evaluation. However, it would benefit you to pay for a professional photographer to take pictures at this point. The photographer can use special cameras and lenses to show the scar most clearly. Duplicates of all pictures, from the time of the injury to the six-month period, should be dated and sent with your demand. Be sure to keep originals and negatives.

The insurance adjuster is probably going to want to meet with you to see the scar. The location and visibility of the scar are crucial in settlement evaluation. If the scar is prominently located on your face and easily visible, your case will naturally be worth more. Your age, appearance, and sex are also important factors. If you are a young, beautiful female, a facial scar is considered particularly traumatic. Conversely, if you are an old, unattractive male, the physical and psychological damages are less.

If you do meet for a viewing with the adjuster, be serious. If you're joking around about the scar, it will seem that you're not really bothered by it. If the scar has seriously affected you emotionally, you should consider seeing a psychologist or psychiatrist for evaluation. Please review the separate chapter in this book on psychological damages.

If the scar is only borderline visible, such as under your hairline, fix yourself up so the scar is most easily seen. Comb your hair back, even if you normally wear it forward. If the scar is located on your leg, wear shorts or a short dress. Be sure to stay out of the sun as much as possible. A suntan can cover up even serious scars.

Don't minimize the settlement value of a visible, permanent scar. Have those free consultations with the lawyers to get some ballpark figures. Many homeowners' policies have at least $100,000 liability coverage. Asking for the policy limits in a serious scar case is certainly not out of line—in fact, depending on the circumstances, $100,000 may not be enough.

Ask the adjuster to give you his top dollar offer without coming down from your policy limit demand. Then go back to the lawyer in whom you had the most confidence. If there's a big gap between the adjuster's top dollar offer and the policy limits, it may pay to hire the lawyer to file suit. Just be sure to work out the kind of deal previously discussed, where the lawyer takes his fee out of whatever he can obtain over the adjuster's offer.

For example, if you have a visible facial scar, your policy limit demand is $100,000, and the adjuster won't offer more than $15,000 or $20,000, a lawsuit may be necessary to get closer to full value. But if the adjuster is already at $60,000 or $70,000, it may not be worthwhile to fight it out in court.

As always, you make the final decision. With the information in this book and the free consultations, you can control your own destiny and your pocketbook.

DOG BITE SETTLEMENT SAMPLE DEMAND LETTER

Today's Date

Your Address and Phone

Re: Date of Accident
Claim # 7777

Dear Adjuster:

As you know, I was visiting John Smith on July 1, 1995. I was swimming in his pool. He was sitting in a lounge chair on the pool deck. I pulled myself up to speak to John. My hand was completely out of the pool. John's dog came right over to me, apparently looking for attention. I reached out to pet the dog when he suddenly jumped at me and bit me on the left cheek.

John called 911. I was taken by ambulance to North County Hospital. Dr. James Serling treated the bite by irrigating it with an antiseptic solution. He gave me a tetanus shot. He also prescribed an antibiotic.

Enclosed are pictures taken the day after the bite. Also enclosed is a picture taken a few months before the incident. As you can see, I had no scars or blemishes on my face.

One week later, I saw Dr. William Martin, a plastic surgeon. The wound was healing but still very obvious. He scheduled a follow-up for November 1995. At that time, he told me the scar would be permanent, but he could do some cosmetic surgery to improve its appearance.

Enclosed is his report, dated November 30, 1995. He states that the surgery could be done as an outpatient in the hospital. His fee would be $3,000, and he approximates hospital and anesthesia fees as an additional $3,000. However, he also states that even with an excellent result, I will still be left with a noticeable scar for the rest of my life.

Also, enclosed are recent pictures, showing my face with a very visible and ugly scar. I am a twenty-five year old single woman. Before this incident, I had a very active social life. I didn't date at all for the first few months after the bite. Recently, I've had a few dates, but I have felt very awkward, self-conscious, and unattractive.

I have had a few visits to Dr. Louis Hedder, a psychiatrist. His reports are enclosed. I've never been to a psychologist or psychiatrist before. I always considered myself to be mentally well-adjusted. Dr. Hedder is recommending extensive psychological testing and counseling. But I just want to try to get on with my life again.

I am enclosing all of my medical bills to date, totalling $3,450. As you know, your company only had a $500 medical payments coverage, which I have already received. Traveler's, my group insurance, has a $2,500 deductible and then pays 80 percent. I am enclosing Traveler's payout sheet, showing total payments of only $760 (80 percent of $950). In addition, enclosed is a letter from Traveler's dated December 15, 1995, which gives notice of a subrogation lien of $760, plus any future payments made. So right now, there is $2,190 in outstanding bills plus $760 I'm going to have to pay back to Traveler's.

I work as a receptionist for A Keyes Co. real estate office. I missed three weeks of work after the accident. Enclosed is the wage loss verification form showing my average gross weekly wage is $360. I had to use up all two weeks of my sick leave and vacation leave time. Therefore, I feel I have lost at least $1,080 in wages. In addition, I feel everybody looks at me funny and treats me differently since I've been back. I'm afraid I might get fired and not be able to get another job because of this damn scar. It's really affected my whole life.

I understand Mr. Smith's homeowner's policy has a liability limit of $100,000. I don't feel that's nearly enough for having to live the rest of my life as a freak. I used to be an attractive and desirable woman. Now, the first thing everybody asks me about is what happened to my face. I would gladly give you all the money and possessions I have to get rid of this thing and be the beautiful woman I used to be. But, since that's not possible, all I can do is ask you for your lousy $100,000 and hope that takes some of my pain away.

I am serious about wanting the $100,000. I feel that's the least you can do. I've talked to several lawyers, and they tell me my case is worth more than that. They say if you don't offer me the $100,000, they can go to court and get a judgment for more, and you'll have to pay because of something called "bad faith." I don't really understand that. But I do know that I'll hire a lawyer if you don't give me what I want.

Please get back to me within twenty days if you want to settle this directly with me.

Sincerely,

Mary Jones

CHAPTER 14

Psychological Damages

Does it pay to be crazy? Lawyers and juries are divided on the answer. Psychological damages can be a major element in some cases, or a relatively minor side issue in others. The cardinal rule discussed at the beginning of the book certainly applies here: don't fake it.

In many ways, psychological injuries are treated just like physical injuries, at least from a legal standpoint. You still need to have expert testimony to prove your case. You can analogize an orthopedic surgeon to a psychiatrist or a chiropractor to a psychologist. The orthopedic surgeon and psychiatrist are both medical doctors specializing in different fields. The chiropractor and psychologist are not medical doctors but are still qualified under the law to testify as experts regarding their treatment of their injured patient, and to render their opinions based on that treatment.

As with physical injuries, pre-existing conditions can be a major issue with psychological damages. If you have had a history of psychiatric treatment or psychoanalysis, the insurance company will take the position that your damages were not caused by the accident. On the other hand, someone with a pre-existing psychological condition can be more vulnerable to a severe aggravation of the problem due to physical trauma. Psychological damage can also be triggered by the stress of lifestyle changes caused by the accident such as the inability to work, constant medical treatment, dealing with attorneys, insurance adjusters, and the court system. Some people handle this stress better than others.

The severity of your physical injury may be a major factor in whether an insurance company or jury believes that you have been psychologically hurt. If your physical injury is relatively minor, you are much less likely to persuade an insurance adjuster that you have been devastated emotionally. Again, it may not take much to trigger emotional damage in someone who is already mentally unstable; however, an adjuster is not likely to place much additional value on a psychological claim where the underlying physical injury is minimal.

There are many different types of claims that come under the general heading of post-traumatic syndrome. One common complaint from car accidents is the fear of driving or of being in an automobile. If the accident occurred on an interstate highway or major road, the injured person may become afraid of driving on that roadway. Some people complain of nightmares, or inability to sleep. Others report an adverse change of personality which affects their personal and business relationships. Accidents are blamed for causing some divorces.

Should you seek psychological help immediately if you are having any problems? Use your common sense. Generally, it depends on the severity and the duration of the problem. A certain amount of anxiety and irritability is normal following a physical injury. But if the accident really upsets you or your problems last longer than a few weeks, you may need professional help.

If you've been to a psychiatrist or psychologist for previous problems, and you were satisfied with your treatment, you should return to the same doctor. This doctor will be in the best position to evaluate what part of your condition is pre-existing and what was aggravated or caused by the accident. Even if you go to a new specialist, your previous doctor's records will be an important aspect in evaluating your claim.

What if you've never seen a psychiatrist or psychologist?

You should be able to get some recommendations as part of your free lawyer consultations, just as you did for the other specialists. You may have to pay up front, even if you have good coverage. If your car insurance personal injury protection pays 80 percent, some specialists will require that you pay the other 20 percent at the time of your visit. Others may require full payment, which means you will have to wait to be reimbursed by your company. Insurance companies may take longer than normal to pay for psychological bills. The company may require more extensive records from the treating doctor, including office notes. In addition, your company may ask you to supply records of previous psychological treatment.

Frequently, a psychologist and psychiatrist will both become involved. You may start with a psychologist. He will have a few consultations with you. Then he will probably evaluate you by having you take a series of psychological tests. If he feels you need prescription medication, he will refer you to a psychiatrist. If you started with a psychiatrist, he may refer you to a psychologist for the extensive standardized testing. These tests can take hours to complete. They are also expensive, frequently costing thousands of dollars. You may want to postpone the tests until you see if your insurance company is paying the bills for the initial evaluations. You certainly don't want to increase your emotional stress by having to pay thousands of dollars out of your pocket.

Usually, the psychologist will recommend that these tests be repeated in six to twelve months. At that time, the doctor may be able to give his opinion on any permanent psychological damage you have suffered from the accident. He may assign a permanent impairment rating, just as the orthopedic surgeon or chiropractor rated you for your physical injuries.

For example, let's say you were terrified of driving following your accident. You had recurring nightmares as well. Eight months later, you are able to drive, but still have considerable anxiety. You only get nightmares once in a while. Your repeat psychological testing confirms that you have improved and healed considerably, but not completely.

The psychologist will review all his findings, from the test results and your regular consultations. His report may cover five to ten pages. In his conclusion, he determines that you have a ten percent permanent psychological impairment as a direct result of the accident.

Will this impairment rating help you obtain a higher settlement? An insurance adjuster will probably evaluate your case slightly higher, assuming everything is legitimate. If your case was worth $15,000 based on your physical injuries, perhaps it will be worth $20,000 based on the additional psychological damage. Was it worth going through eight to ten months of treatment for an extra $5,000? Hopefully, the treatment helped you recover, become better adjusted, and more able to cope with your problems following the accident. If so, that $5,000 is just the icing on the cake. Peace of mind is worth more than any amount of money.

CHAPTER 15

Firing Lawyers

Let's assume you decided to hire a lawyer for your simple car accident case. You worked out a deal where the lawyer receives a fee of 30 percent of any amount over $15,000, which was the offer you got on your own. The lawyer tells you he's going to see how much he can get without a lawsuit. If it's not enough, he says he will go to court.

You don't hear anything for a month—no phone calls, no letters. Then he calls and tells you he's got the insurance company up to $20,000, which is supposedly a final offer. He's recommending you take it. He says: "My fee will only be $1,500; which is 30 percent of $5,000. So you'll be coming out with an extra $3,500 in just a month by hiring me. In reviewing your case, I really think you'd be better off taking it than throwing the dice and going to court."

What do you do? I think you know that I'm not going to tell you to take the money and run, no questions asked. But I'm not going to tell you to fire the lawyer right away either, even if that is the title of this chapter.

The first thing you need is a lot more information. You need to get that information by communicating with your lawyer. Lack of communication is the number one reason that clients fire lawyers. Common complaints include: "He never returned my phone calls." Or, "I never knew what was happening with my case." Or, "He didn't explain the law to me and how it applies to my case."

It takes two to communicate. Lawyers certainly have a continuing responsibility to keep their clients informed. But clients also need to assert themselves. Don't be afraid to ask questions.

Let's go back to the situation I described at the beginning of this chapter. I said that you hired a lawyer after getting an offer of $15,000 on your own. Then you heard nothing from him for one month. It is your responsibility to let the lawyer know, right from the beginning, what you want and expect. You should make it clear that he must have your consent before he makes any offers or counteroffers.

How did he get the insurance company to come up from $15,000 to $20,000? Did he use the negotiating technique of getting something for nothing? Perhaps he said this to the adjuster, "I've just been hired. I know you offered my client $15,000. We both know the case is worth more. Tell me what you can settle for right now, before I file suit."

Perhaps the adjuster responded, "Okay. My maximum authority is $20,000. That's absolutely all I've got. And I'm only offering it all to you now because we've done business before, and I respect you and your firm."

You are entitled to know these important details of your lawyer's negotiating. Most clients just care about the bottom line. Hopefully, what you've learned in this book will help you realize that you have it in your power to improve that bottom line, whether you're handling it yourself, or with the help of a lawyer. When a client and lawyer are working together, with open and honest communication, the most successful results are bound to occur.

Now let's say that open communication is lacking. Your lawyer, without your knowledge or consent, decided to come down from the $50,000 policy limit you had demanded. He tells the adjuster, "I know you offered $15,000 to my client, so I've got to make the next move. I'll split the difference between the fifty policy limits and your $15,000 offer. I can settle the case today for $32,500. But this will only be open until suit is filed. If we can't settle now, I'll be looking for fifty or more in litigation."

The adjuster responds, "Okay. I'll give you my maximum authority—$20,000. You might as well take it, because filing suit won't change it."

So then your lawyer comes to you and recommends accepting the $20,000. Was he unethical in reducing the demand to $32,500 without at least discussing it with you? There are thick books of ethical rules that lawyers must follow. Local and state bar associations have special lawyers who interpret the rules and give advice to practicing lawyers. There are many gray areas. This situation may be one of them.

But even if this lawyer's conduct was ethical, it certainly exhibited a lack of respect for you, the client. And, it also showed a total lack of communication, which is exactly what makes clients angry enough to switch lawyers.

You say to him, "How could you come down to $32,500 without telling me first?"

He says, "I thought that's why you hired me—to use my own judgment, experience, and discretion to get you the best recovery."

You say, "Yeah, but this is my case. Shouldn't I make the final decision?"

You are absolutely right. It is your case, and you should make the final decision, not only on the settlement, but also on all the offers and counteroffers along the way. But if you didn't make that clear to your lawyer from the start, then you are also guilty of poor communication.

You can't assume that your lawyer is going to read your mind. Many lawyers are used to clients that just automatically go along with whatever the lawyer does. Some lawyers are even offended when a client has the audacity to question the lawyer's advice and actions. This is similar to a doctor who won't listen to a patient's self-diagnosis, because the doctor is the expert. After all, the patient didn't go to medical school, and the client didn't go to law school.

But I think the nineties is about asserting yourself. It's your body. You know more about it than any doctor, because you've lived in it your whole life. And it's your case. You've gone through the pain and suffering since the first day it happened. You're the one who has the lost wages, the unpaid medical bills, the credit cards that suddenly get out of control. So you are entitled to be an active participant in your case. That means not just putting in your two cents, but being at least an equal partner, or even having a 51 percent controlling interest.

So don't fire your lawyer if you've been letting him run the show all the way and then suddenly you are not pleased with how it comes out. However, if you have made it clear from the beginning that you want to be actively involved in the entire process, and your lawyer continues to ignore you, then you've got a real problem.

Try to solve communication problems the moment they appear. Let's say you've left three phone messages in three days and haven't got a call back. Or you've received no correspondence from your lawyer since you hired him three or four weeks ago. Schedule another meeting. Tell his secretary you *must* see him personally. If you express yourself better in writing, send him a certified letter expressing your concerns and needs.

If letters, phone calls, and meetings don't work, then you've got to consider switching lawyers. A change in lawyers may also be necessary if you have a great difference of opinion on the value of your case. In our example, your lawyer is advising you to settle for $20,000. You believe that your case is worth $30,000 to $40,000. He has already reduced the demand, without your knowledge, to $32,500. It's time for a change.

So, how do you go about firing a lawyer and getting a new one? And what happens when you do switch?

If your first lawyer has not yet filed a lawsuit, it's a lot easier. Find your new lawyer. This lawyer agrees with your evaluation. He's willing to get involved in litigation to maximize the recovery. He promises to keep you posted by sending you copies of all correspondence. He tells you he will always consult with you before negotiating, and that you have the final say. These are the actions that result in a successful lawyer-client relationship.

Now, what about the first lawyer? Usually, your new lawyer will have a standard form letter that he will ask you to sign, similar to the following:

SAMPLE LETTER TO SWITCH LAWYERS

Your Address and Phone Today's Date

Re: Date of Accident

Dear Attorney:

Please be advised that I have decided to retain new counsel. My new lawyer is ______________.

Please send a complete copy of my file to the following:

(Name and address of New Law Firm)

If you wish to discuss this further, please call Attorney ______________ at the following number: (New lawyer's phone number).

Sincerely,

(Your signature)

By sending such a letter, you avoid the uncomfortable situation of firing the lawyer on the phone or in person. In addition, your intention is in writing with your new lawyer's name, address, and phone number. Since a lawsuit has not yet been filed, you do not need a judge's approval. (We'll discuss litigation cases shortly.) However, even without a lawsuit, switching lawyers is not quite so easy.

Remember the chapter where we discussed subrogation liens? That's where you had to pay back Medicare, your group health insurance carrier, or your worker's compensation carrier. Depending on the amount of your settlement, you tried to negotiate the sum so that you gave each carrier as little as possible. When you fire a lawyer, he's usually entitled to a lien for "the reasonable value of his services."

You can be sure that your first lawyer is not going to be thrilled. He's going to write a letter to the insurance company, putting them on notice that he's entitled to a lien on your settlement, and that his name should be on any settlement check. Most insurance companies will honor such a letter.

Where does that leave you? Unfortunately, it leaves many clients in a position where they end up paying double fees. What happens too often is that the first lawyer's fees are added on to the second lawyer's fees. Both lawyers get paid, and the client ends up with substantially less in his pocket. What went wrong?

Let's assume that your second lawyer, with your knowledge and consent, ends up settling for $35,000. Your second lawyer, like your first, agreed to 30 percent of any recovery over $15,000. Assume that your first lawyer had $2,000 in costs. Look at charts D, E, F, and G to see some of the possibilities in dividing up that $35,000 pie with two lawyers involved.

SAMPLE SETTLEMENT STATEMENTS WITH TWO LAWYERS INVOLVED

Chart D

Gross:	$35,000
Less Second Lawyer's fee (30 percent of recovery over $15,000 = 30 percent of $20,000)	– 6,000
	$29,000
Less First Lawyer's fee (Same basis: 30 percent over $15,000	– 6,000
	$23,000
Less costs	– 2,000
Net to you	$21,000

Chart E

Gross:	$35,000
Less Second Lawyer's fee (same as chart D)	– 6,000
	$29,000
Less First Lawyer's fee (30 percent of recovery over $15,000 when he was representing you. Since he got you $20,000, he gets 30 percent of $5,000)	– 1,500
	$27,500
Less costs	– 2,000
Net to you	$25,500

Chart F

Gross:	$35,000
Less Second Lawyer's fee	– 6,000
(same as Charts D & E)	$29,000
Less First Lawyer's fee (Based on hourly rate for time he represented you. He claims 20 hours at $200 hour)	– 4,000
	$25,000
Less costs	– 2,000
Net to you	$23,000

Chart G

Gross:	$35,000
Less Lawyers' fees: 30 percent of recovery over $15,000 = 30 percent of $20,000. *To be divided between both lawyers*	
2nd lawyer's fees:	4,500
1st lawyer's fees:	1,500
(total fees)	– 6,000
	$29,000
Less costs	– 2,000
Net to you	$27,000

As you can see, the gross settlement and the costs remain constant. All that changes is how much the lawyers are getting and how much you're getting. Obviously, you strongly prefer the bottom line in Chart G. But you're not likely to obtain that sum without negotiating for it as a condition to hiring Lawyer number 2.

You must tell Lawyer number 2 the following:

"I don't care what Lawyer number 1 gets. That's *your* problem. Any fee lawyer number 1 gets must come out of your total fee, lawyer number 2. I bargained with lawyer number 1 to give him a fee of 30 percent of any recovery over $15,000. I will not be penalized for switching lawyers. If you agree, please make it clear in our written contingent fee contract."

If lawyer number 2 wants your case, he will go along with the above arrangement. Then it will be in his best interest to bargain lawyer number 1 to the lowest reasonable fee possible, because it's coming out of lawyer number 2's pocket. In charts D, E, and F, lawyer number 1's fee came out of your pocket. Even with chart E, you're giving up an extra $1,500; in effect, that's your penalty, or extra legal fee, for changing lawyers. It may be ethical (another one of those many gray areas), but it surely isn't fair to you.

Therefore, if you ever switch lawyers in any type of contingency fee case, be sure that your new lawyer agrees in writing to reduce his own fee by the amount of the first lawyer's fee. You and your new lawyer should each sign and receive a copy of this agreement.

In cases where you change lawyers after a lawsuit has been filed, you should still follow this procedure when signing your contingency fee contract with the new lawyer. However, your new lawyer must get court approval to be substituted as your new counsel of record. In some states, a hearing is required, and you may need to testify. In other states, the two lawyers sign a stipulation for substitution of counsel and the presiding judge generally approves it without a hearing.

Your first lawyer will probably file a notice of lien in the lawsuit to be sure that his fee is paid. But if you've already agreed in writing with your new lawyer as I've recommended, you're not likely to have a problem. On some occasions, the first and second lawyer can't agree on the amount of the first lawyer's fee. In those instances, some type of proceeding may be required, such as mediation, arbitration, or a lawsuit. But whatever the first lawyer is awarded, at least you know it's going to come out of the second lawyer's pocket, not yours.

CHAPTER 16

Cases Where You Would Be Wise to Hire a Lawyer

There are specialized types of personal injury cases where representing yourself could prove unwise, and possibly disastrous. I will discuss these briefly along with the steps you should take to be sure that you and your lawyer have the best possible case, and you get the best deal on attorney's fees.

Product Liability

If you are seriously injured due to a defective product, you may have a product liability case. Naturally, if your injury was your own fault, you probably do not have a case. Generally, a manufacturer is only liable if the product is the direct cause of your injury.

If you are misusing the product, the manufacturer will probably not be liable; however, a good lawyer may be able to prove that the manufacturer should have been able to predict or foresee that a consumer would use the product the way you used it.

The defect can be in the way the product was designed, or in the way it was built. Sometimes, a manufacturer can be held liable for failure to give proper instructions on using the product, or failure to give an adequate warning about the dangers.

You will need to consult a lawyer who specializes in product liability cases. You and the lawyer will be taking on a big company with a lot of money. These types of cases involve the hiring of many different experts. There is no way that you can fight equally on your own against these companies. First of all, you won't know what experts to hire. Even if you did, you probably wouldn't have the money to pay the experts.

If you try to settle the case on your own, the company is likely to deny liability, or offer you a nuisance value settlement, even if you have a serious injury. Most big companies would rather pay their lawyers to fight a product liability case, if they feel they have a good chance to win. Winning such cases will dissuade others from trying to make a similar claim.

Therefore, you should find a product liability lawyer. The sooner you hire a lawyer in this type of case, the better. A good lawyer will want to do a preliminary investigation as soon as possible after the accident. Contact your local bar association to get the names of specialists in this area.

You can negotiate his contingency fee as we have previously discussed in chapter 8. (Also, see chapter 16, section 3 Negotiating With Your Lawyer.) Be sure the lawyer is taking the case strictly on a contingency basis. Also make sure that the lawyer advances *all* costs and will not ask you to pay the costs if you lose the case. This condition should be added in writing to the contingent fee agreement. The last thing you need is your own lawyer turning against you and suing you for many thousands of dollars in costs, after you lose a case.

There are also some important steps to take as soon as the injury occurs. Be sure to keep possession of the product which injured you. Keep the product in exactly the same condition. Have pictures taken of the product, the injuries caused by it, and the area in which the accident occurred. Hold on to the receipt, or try to get a receipt where you purchased it. If you charged it, keep a copy of your itemized credit card bill.

If you have the original box and any instruction sheets, pamphlets or diagrams, keep them with the product. If these items have been discarded, but the same item and container is still available, purchase a new one and keep it with the defective product. This will be important in proving whether there were adequate warnings of the dangers, or clear and complete instructions for use.

Naturally, you need to go to an emergency room and obtain complete follow-up medical treatment, just as we discussed earlier in the car accident case. Be sure to tell all doctors the complete details of how the accident happened. Include the name and description of the product which injured you. This is very important to prove that this particular product was the direct cause of your injury.

If you follow these steps, you have an excellent chance of a successful recovery. There is a much greater likelihood of a lawsuit than in an auto accident or slip and fall case. However, if you and your lawyer do your jobs, and the manufacturer realizes that you've got a strong case, you should be able to obtain a very reasonable settlement without going to trial.

Medical Malpractice

A medical malpractice claim is probably the most complicated and difficult of all the personal injury cases. Most states have comprehensive laws which require that various legal and technical steps be taken before, and during, a lawsuit for a medical malpractice case. The statute of limitations for filing a malpractice lawsuit is usually only one or two years, compared to three to four years for other personal injury cases. In addition, it is very rare that a malpractice case will be settled without a lawsuit. Why? A hospital or doctor will not usually admit negligence or malpractice. And most doctors will not testify against other doctors, especially physicians who practice in the same community.

Therefore, it is almost impossible to settle a medical malpractice case without hiring a lawyer. As mentioned in the product liability section, a specialist in this area is essential. Unlike product liability cases, it is difficult to know if you even have a legitimate malpractice case.

There are three basic parts to a medical malpractice case:

negligence, causation, and serious damages. Malpractice is a fancy word for medical negligence. Malpractice is defined as falling below the normal standard of care; in other words, a doctor, hospital, or other medical provider fails to do what other similar specialists would do under similar circumstances. This is only the first part of a possible case, and it is very difficult to prove.

Just having a bad result does not mean malpractice. If you have surgery, and you end up worse than you were before, you may just have had a bad result. If the standard of care for your condition indicated surgery as a reasonable treatment, and the doctor performed the surgery properly, you probably don't have a case.

However, let's assume the doctor did fall below the normal standard of care. Let's say the doctor did something he wasn't supposed to do, or didn't do something he was supposed to do. Also assume your lawyer can get qualified doctors in the same specialty to testify against your doctor. Even then you still only have the first part of your case.

The second and third parts are causation and serious damages. Let's assume your doctor fails to diagnose your condition properly. You are a tennis player, and you are having pain in your shoulder. Your doctor briefly examines you, takes no X rays or other diagnostic tests and says it's just an inflammation. He prescribes some anti-inflammatory medication and tells you to stop playing tennis for a few weeks. You take the medication, do not play tennis, and still have the pain a month later. You see the doctor again. He tells you to keep taking the medication. Nothing more.

You see a second doctor who takes X rays and performs an MRI scan. Both the X rays and the scan show a tumor. The second doctor performs surgery and removes the tumor. Tests show the tumor is not cancer. After a short time, you're fine and back to playing tennis.

Did your first doctor commit malpractice? Yes, he did. He failed to perform standard diagnostic procedures such as X rays and MRI scans. He was particularly negligent for failing to do any follow-up work after you did not improve in one month.

Do you have a malpractice case? No, you probably don't. Why? The doctor's negligence did not cause you a serious injury. Your second doctor gave you the proper care. Your tumor was diagnosed, and the surgery cured your problem. The only damages you could claim that were the direct result of the negligence were your pain and suffering for the month following the misdiagnosis. You could also claim the amount of the first doctor's bills for two office visits. These damages are not really serious enough to warrant a malpractice case, which will most likely cost many thousands of dollars and take years in litigation.

In these kinds of situations, where there is negligence which does not cause serious injury, you do have an option. You can contact that first doctor who was clearly negligent. Show him your subsequent medical records, including the X rays, MRI films, hospital records, and surgeon's reports. Ask him for a small amount of money to cover your out-of-pocket expenses—whatever your insurance didn't cover, plus a little bit more for your pain and suffering. Tell him you'll forget about a lawyer, and you'll sign a release.

Doctors usually have a large deductible on their malpractice insurance. The deductibles generally range from $5,000 to $50,000. In some clear-cut malpractice situations, the doctor may pay you a few thousand out of his pocket, even if his negligence did not cause you serious injury. He may do it because he realizes he made a mistake. Perhaps he's worried about having to pay more if you find a lawyer who will represent you. Or maybe he is afraid that you will report him to his local medical association. Such a report usually requires a hearing. At the very least, this will inconvenience him and taint his reputation.

Remember, I am only recommending that you try to settle without a lawyer if you were not seriously injured by the negligence. Let's go back to our example. Let's assume that the tumor in your shoulder is malignant. By the time the second doctor diagnoses it, the cancer has spread to other parts of your body. Now you have a life-threatening illness.

The key issue is did the delay in diagnosis *cause* a serious injury? If the first doctor had diagnosed it right away, would your cancer have spread beyond your shoulder? If the diagnosis had been made immediately, could you have been cured? The failure to diagnose cancer quickly enough is a common potential basis for a malpractice case. In this situation, you must contact several malpractice lawyers as quickly as possible.

As discussed in the product liability section, be sure the lawyer you hire specializes in malpractice cases. Also be sure the lawyer will handle your claim strictly on a contingency fee, will advance all costs, and will not hold you responsible for costs if you lose. If you are not sure whether you have the three elements of a malpractice case—negligence, causation, and serious injuries—obtain free consultations from malpractice lawyers. Do this as soon as you suspect you have a case. Waiting too long can ruin even the strongest medical malpractice claim.

Worker's Compensation

When you are injured while working at your job, you probably have a worker's compensation case. Every state has worker's compensation laws. These laws give the worker certain benefits under certain circumstances. However, the laws also take away the worker's right to sue his employer, even if the injury was the employer's fault. The worker's compensation laws do not prevent the worker from suing somebody else who was at fault.

For example, suppose you are a courier. You are on your way to deliver a package. You are driving your company vehicle. While stopped at a red light, you are rear-ended by another driver. Now you have two possible cases: a worker's compensation claim, and a third party claim against the other driver.

You should proceed to follow all of the advice in this book pertaining to auto accidents. But you will also need to consult lawyers specializing in worker's compensation. In some states, you may discover it is better for you to just pursue the third party claim and forget about worker's compensation.

For example, in Florida you can get your medical bills paid by your own insurance company for your private car, even though you were driving a company car. This will allow you to choose your own doctors, instead of having to see the company's doctors.

Also, if your worker's compensation pays for your medical bills, there will be a lien on any settlement with the other driver's insurance company.

If you are injured at work, and no one else is involved except you and your employer, you will probably be limited to worker's compensation benefits. Most states have a system that allows the worker to collect benefits without hiring a lawyer. These benefits include payment of medical bills and some compensation for the time you are out of work.

So, if you can get the benefits without a lawyer, why do you need one? As with medical malpractice and product liability, worker's compensation is a specialized and technical area of law. Most likely, without a lawyer, you may not get all the benefits to which you are entitled.

For example, the majority of systems base your compensation on a percentage of your average weekly wage. This percentage is referred to as your compensation rate or "comp rate." Many employers will just figure your regular weekly salary as your average weekly wage. Some employers may base it on your net, or take-home pay.

But, under your state law, in figuring your average weekly wage, you may be entitled to include some or all of the following: your gross (before deductions) salary, including overtime, expense allowances for travel, meals, and entertainment, group health insurance benefits, pension plan benefits, and even the value of such miscellaneous items as uniforms or a company car used for personal purposes. Only an experienced worker's compensation lawyer will know how to get you the highest possible average weekly wage resulting in the best possible comp rate.

A lawyer can also get you reimbursement for past benefits you didn't receive, or force payment to doctors who helped you, but were not authorized to treat you. In addition, depending on the state, a lawyer may be able to obtain a lump sum or "washout" settlement which would not have been offered to you otherwise.

The lawyer may also be able to get his fee paid in addition to the benefits he obtains for you. Be sure to discuss the possibility of an award of attorney's fees when you have your free consultations with the worker's compensation lawyers. You should still be able to use the negotiating techniques discussed in previous chapters to get the best possible deal with your lawyer. For example, if you have been offered certain compensation benefits without the lawyer, he should only base his contingency fee on the additional benefits he is able to get you. And if he obtains an award of attorney's fees, you should not have to pay any fee out of your benefits.

The strategy we discussed earlier should always guide you. The more free consultations you get, the clearer your rights will be. The more knowledge you obtain about your potential benefits, including attorney's fees, the better position you will be in to make yourself a good deal. Remember, like most things in life, lawyers are negotiable. The worst that can happen when you ask for a better deal is that you will be given no for an answer. In cases where you need a lawyer, use the techniques suggested in this book and you will still save a lot of money.

Death Cases

Your loved one is killed in an accident. It's a tragedy I hope you never experience. But if it happens, you should hire a lawyer as quickly as possible.

Emotionally, you will be traumatized and depressed. You will have to be planning the funeral. You'll be receiving condolence visits and sympathy calls. But in the midst of all this, try to find a lawyer.

Each state has it's own wrongful death statute. A wrongful death simply means that someone else was at fault. These wrongful death statutes specify the damages that can be claimed and the statute of limitations period. Frequently, the statute of limitations is shorter than in a standard personal injury case. For example, a typical wrongful death statute of limitations may be one to two years, compared to three or four years for a personal injury claim. This is one important reason to find a lawyer quickly.

Once the lawyer is hired, he should initiate a thorough investigation. This may include a private investigator, accident reconstruction expert, and engineer. In your initial interview with the lawyer, learn his plan of action. If he intends to rely completely on police reports and other public investigations, you may want to look for somebody else.

A death case almost always requires money for experts—money that is worth spending. The private investigator will track down witnesses and get their recorded statements while events are still fresh in their minds. He'll take pictures of the accident site and the vehicles involved.

If the death was the result of a car accident, be absolutely sure you keep possession of the car. Don't make any repairs, or change it in any way. Keep it in your own garage if possible. This will keep it safe and avoid large storage charges. If you don't have a garage, perhaps a relative or good friend will help you out. If you must use a storage facility, find one indoors and with good security. However, be aware that the case may be pending for years, and storage charges can really add up.

If you do not own the car, appeal to the compassion of the owner. Offer to purchase the car if at all possible. If the owner will not sell it, offer to pay for storage charges; however, the owner must promise not to repair it.

Why is it so important to keep possession of the car? It is a crucial piece of evidence in the case. The accident reconstruction expert will look at the car to determine how fast the vehicles were going, where the impact occurred, and what happened to the car after impact. The engineer may be a biomechanical expert. He will try to figure out which part of the accident caused which injuries. He may even determine that the car was negligently designed and that the design defect contributed to the death.

The defense experts will also be entitled to inspect the car. Their inspections may occur much later, when a lawsuit has already been filed. It's important that they view the car in the same condition as your own experts.

The wrongful death statute in your state will specify what types of damages you can recover. Keep all funeral bills, and bills from all medical treatment following tne accident. Get written estimates for repair or replacement of the car, or any other damaged personal property. These are clear-cut expenses. But other damages are less obvious.

Advise your attorney of any possible way which your deceased love one financially contributed to your support. If the deceased was a working spouse, locate all recent tax returns and pay stubs. But what if you have lost an unmarried adult son or daughter?

In one instance, I represented the parents of a recently divorced twenty-five-year-old man. The young man was tragically killed in a plane crash. He had no children. Just before he died, he had a meeting with his parents and their new landlady. The landlady was concerned about the ability of the parents to pay for their new apartment. The son told the landlady that he was planning to live with his parents and contribute half the rent, and pay for half the utilities bills. He left some of his personal items in the apartment. He promised to move in with the rest of his stuff after his plane trip. He never signed the lease or had any written agreement with his parents or the landlady. He never actually contributed any money before his death.

In most states, the damages that parents can recover for the death of an unmarried adult are very limited. However, economic loss is almost always allowable. In the case above, I was able to get a sworn affidavit from the landlady confirming the facts of the meeting. Her testimony was sufficient to prove that the parents had suffered a substantial economic loss when their son died. The economic loss was half of the parents' rent and utility bills for the rest of their lives. The anticipated length of their lives was based on standard mortality tables.

The broad and vague element of pain and suffering is particularly difficult in a death case. Generally, a surviving spouse or parents of a minor will be able to claim pain and suffering. Try to put together for your lawyer a chronological family album. If you have lost your spouse, include pictures and videos that start when your relationship began. If you have lost your child, begin with the first baby pictures. Record a narrative explaining the pictures and video. Express your feelings as you relive all the precious moments in your life. This can be an emotionally draining experience, but it can also be a good release for you. It will be very helpful to your lawyer in settlement negotiations or in trial, if it goes that far.

How can any one put a monetary value on a human life? The wrongful death statutes do provide specific guidelines. But when someone you love has been lost forever, no amount of money can bring that person back. This is one time where you need an experienced lawyer to be objective. Give the lawyer everything you can to prove how much your loved one meant to you. Let the lawyer do the rest.

Minors

1. General Guidelines

If your injured child is under eighteen, you will probably need a lawyer. Most states have laws requiring that a guardianship be set up for a settlement involving a minor. The guardianship is a specialized legal procedure that a lawyer should handle. Many states also require that a judge approve the terms of a minor settlement. This also requires a lawyer's involvement.

You may not need a guardianship or a judge's approval. In some states, the amount of the total settlement may be the determining factor, or the net amount received by the minor.

Obtain several free consultations with lawyers at the beginning of the case. Be sure you are clear about the requirements of a guardianship or court proceeding in your state. Ask the lawyers if there are any special restrictions on attorney's fees for minors. Some states may have statutes which specify maximum contingent fees under certain circumstances. If your state doesn't have such a law, the lawyer may still be more willing than usual to reduce his fee. He will be concerned if he needs to get court approval for the settlement.

Some judges take a special interest in looking at what is best for the minor. If court approval is required, the judge probably has the power to order a reduction in the attorney's fee. The lawyer may have already had experience with fee reductions by certain judges. For example, one judge may have a standard policy that he will not approve any minor settlement unless the attorney's fee is 25 percent or less.

Therefore, if you do hire a lawyer, be willing to negotiate really hard to get the lowest possible contingent fee. Also, if a guardianship is required, look for a lawyer who will do the guardianship work at no additional charge. This should include any annual accountings to be filed with the court.

In some states, the judge may appoint a guardian *ad litem.* This may be more likely where there is a very large settlement involved. The guardian *ad litem* is usually a lawyer who is on a court list for these types of cases. In effect, he is appointed specifically to protect the best interests of the minor. In that role, this lawyer can become the adversary of the parents and the lawyer hired by the parents.

Let's assume you are the parents of an eight-year-old boy. The three of you are in your car, stopped at a red light. You are rear-ended by a vehicle. The other driver speeds away before you can even get his license plate number.

You only own the one car. You have uninsured motorist coverage of $100,000 single limits. This means that, regardless of how many people are injured in your car, the insurance company is only responsible for a total of $100,000.

There were no witnesses to the accident. There is no way to track down the hit-and-run driver. Therefore, you are entitled to make a claim under your uninsured motorist coverage.

All three of you are badly injured. You are taken by ambulance to the hospital. All of you require regular treatment by several doctors. The father's MRI scan reveals a herniated disc in the back. The mother's MRI shows a neck herniation. Neither of you had previous neck or back problems. Your son suffered a broken nose, broken right wrist, and multiple lacerations on his face requiring stitches. He will have permanent facial scars.

You get several free legal consultations. You determine that, in your state, a guardianship proceeding is required, if the minor's net settlement exceeds $5,000. The case must be filed in the probate court. The probate judge has complete jurisdiction, including approval of the terms of the settlement. There is no need to file in the probate court until a settlement has been reached.

Under these circumstances, is it necessary to hire a lawyer right away? Most lawyers reading this will say, "Of course it is. A lawyer needs to be involved immediately, especially if the state has any provisions for bad faith in uninsured motorist cases. If so, you've got to set up the insurance company for a possible bad faith claim." However, you may be able to do some of the work yourself and save a lot in attorney's fees.

Remember when we discussed bad faith? Basically, bad faith means the insurance company, given a reasonable opportunity, fails to settle within policy limits a case that is clearly worth more. Then, if a jury awards more than the policy limits, the insurance company may have to pay the full verdict.

Some states allow for bad faith claims in all personal injury claims. Other states may not provide for bad faith if you're making an uninsured motorist claim against your own company. In your free consultations, be sure you determine if you've got a chance for bad faith and under what circumstances. Be completely up front about your intentions in these consultations. The conversation may go something like this:

YOU: All three of us are badly injured. There's only $100,000 single limit, uninsured motorist coverage. I plan to ask for the policy limits. If my insurance company doesn't give us the full $100,000, I'm going to hire a lawyer.

LAWYER: I understand you think you can do some of this yourself, but you would really be making a mistake in this case. We have a legitimate chance for bad faith here. But bad faith is very tricky and complicated. There are so many things we need to do to prepare the file properly.

YOU: Do you think there's a good chance my insurance company may offer the full policy limits if I ask for it?

LAWYER: Yes, there's a chance. But....

YOU: And isn't it true that there can't be any bad faith unless the insurance company has had a reasonable opportunity to settle for the policy limits?

LAWYER: Yes, that's basically true. But. . . .

YOU: So why should I hire you now if the insurance company is going to end up offering the $100,000, whether you're my lawyer or not?

LAWYER: Because if they don't offer the full $100,000, we want the stage set for the bad faith claim.

YOU: Exactly. And that's when I want to hire you. If my company offers us less than the $100,000, I want you to work on a contingency based on that. Will you take a percentage of anything over what we've already been offered? That way, we can put that offer in our back pocket.

LAWYER: I don't like it, naturally. But obviously, you're determined to do this. So get back to me after they've made an offer, and we'll talk more about it then.

YOU: Okay. At least you're open to the possibility of working with me. Now, when should I make the policy limit demand? And how long a time limit should I give the insurance company to come up with the policy limits?

LAWYER: I really don't feel comfortable advising you about these matters. This is strictly a free consultation. I'm not representing you at this point.

YOU: Look, you know I intend to make the initial policy limit demand. You know that if I don't get the full amount, I'm going to need a lawyer. Don't you want me to come back to you with the best chance for you to help me?

LAWYER: Okay. Here's what you want to do. Wait until your wife, your son, and you have all been discharged by the doctors. Get all the hospital and medical records, including final reports. Send everything, including pictures, to your insurance company. Be sure you have extra sets of pictures for us. Give them thirty days to settle for the policy limits. We've had cases that have held that ten or fifteen days isn't enough time. Twenty days is a gray area. But thirty days should be more than enough, especially since the company has already had so much time to evaluate the case and set its reserves during your treatment. Send the demand letter certified, return receipt. If they offer you less than the $100,000, see me right away. If they don't make any offer within the thirty days, see me on the thirty-first day. That's it.

YOU: I really appreciate this. Now, what percentage would you take over any offer they make?

LAWYER: It's premature to discuss that. Come back to me immediately after they make the offer and then we'll decide.

YOU: Fair enough. Unless they offer me the $100,000, I'll be back.

LAWYER: You'd make a good lawyer, you know that?

YOU: Thanks.

2. Negotiating With the Adjuster

Let's assume that you follow the lawyer's advice. You send final reports from the doctors and pictures of your child's permanent scar. You demand the $100,000 single policy limits. You give the company thirty days.

On the twenty-first day, you get a call from the insurance adjuster.

ADJUSTER: We received your demand. We really don't have everything we need to fully evaluate the case. For example, you haven't sent us the emergency room records for any of you. We also don't have the plastic surgeon's bills for your son. However, we wanted to show good faith and respond within thirty days. So, at this time, I'm making an offer as follows: $15,000 for you, $15,000 for your wife, and $25,000 for your son. Based on what we have, I think $55,000 total is fair.

YOU: I was told by some lawyers that our claims together are worth more than $100,000.

ADJUSTER: Well, we don't see it that way. However, if you're willing to come down from the $100,000, I've got a little more room to negotiate.

YOU: Could you send me a letter with your offer? In fact, I'm at the office now. Here's my FAX number ______. Could you FAX me something today? I need to discuss it with my wife tonight.

ADJUSTER: Well, the secretaries are backed up. I could just FAX you a handwritten note with my offer. I'll send you a more detailed letter with the additional items we need.

YOU: Fine. Thanks.

ADJUSTER: Now, please get back to me as soon as possible. I'd like to wrap this up.

YOU: Okay.

Let's analyze this hypothetical conversation. Read between the lines. What was the adjuster really saying? He responded well before the thirty-day limit. He made an initial offer of $55,000. He clearly states he's negotiable. In his mind, he's operating in good faith.

But he also wants to settle the case as quickly as possible for less than the $100,000 policy limits. He wants you to commit yourself to a counteroffer of less than the $100,000. And he certainly is anxious to settle with you directly. He doesn't want a lawyer to be involved. He knows that a lawyer will probably file a lawsuit. With a lawyer involved, he figures he will have to give up the $100,000, and possibly more if bad faith can be proven.

He also divided the settlement offer. He knows that your son's claim will have to be approved by the court. That's one reason he offered your son the most. Of course, with permanent facial scars on an eight-year-old, it's clear that your son's case is the strongest. You and your wife may have had the herniations before the accident, even though you had no previous problems. But your son's scars are definitely accident-related. Depending on how visible the scars are, your son's case alone might be worth $100,000. So, the adjuster is hoping to save his company some money. But he may actually have authority to settle for the $100,000, if necessary.

In our hypothetical conversation, you were very smart. You have learned your lessons well from our previous chapters. You didn't come down from the $100,000; in fact, you said that lawyers told you the claims were worth more than $100,000. You made it clear that you expected the full $100,000. You also alerted the adjuster to the fact that you've already consulted lawyers. The adjuster can infer that you may hire a lawyer, especially if you don't get $100,000 on your own.

You were also astute in requesting that the adjuster FAX you his offer immediately. Now you have a dated document which you can take to the lawyer right away. If your lawyer ends up filing suit and ultimately going after the insurance company for bad faith, the faxed offer will be a crucial piece of evidence.

It's also clear from the adjuster's language that he has a lot more authority than $55,000. He prefaces his offer with "at this time." These words imply that a higher offer is forthcoming.

The adjuster asks you for some additional documentation. He specifically mentions emergency room records and plastic surgeon's bills. He also tells you that he will send you a letter with the additional items he needs. Apparently, the insurance company wants other items besides the emergency room records and plastic surgeon's bills—note that the adjuster used the words "for example" before itemizing specific needs.

The letter he sends you could also be important in a case involving bad faith. A jury would have to decide whether the missing items were really necessary to evaluate the case. Your lawyer would argue that they already had more than enough evidence and time to realize that the claims together were worth more than $100,000.

3. Negotiating With Your Lawyer

So, you contact the lawyer right after you get the faxed offer. He tells you to come right in. You bring your wife this time. You both know that there is a good chance you'll hire the lawyer, if he's willing to make the deal you want on attorney's fees. The lawyer sees that you are both serious. He knows that he may well get at least $100,000 without a lot of work. He knows that you will not hire him if he doesn't reduce his normal fee. And he also knows that a judge will be closely examining his fee on your son's settlement.

Bring copies of your complete file to this meeting. If you hire the lawyer, you can leave everything with him. Here's how the meeting might play out.

YOU: I listened to everything you told me to do. You can see, I gave the company thirty days. They offered the $55,000 yesterday, on the twenty-first day.

LAWYER: You did a nice job.

YOU: Thanks. Where do we go from here?

LAWYER: If I'm going to represent you, time is of the essence. We've got eight days before the end of your thirty-day time limit demand. I'll FAX the adjuster a letter of representation and tell him we're firm on the $100,000. If he doesn't come up with it in eight days, we file suit in nine days.

YOU: What about your fee?

LAWYER: Okay. You want me to take my percentage on what I can get over $55,000. The only problem is, we're going to need court approval on your son's settlement. So we'll need a separate fee agreement for him.

YOU: What are you proposing?

LAWYER: I normally charge 33 1/3 percent without a suit and 40 percent once a suit is filed. What I'll do here is this: If the adjuster comes up with the $100,000 in the next 8 days, I'll take 33 1/3 percent over the $15,000 settlements already offered to you and your wife. For your son, I'll just take 25 percent of the total settlement allotted to him.

YOU: Wait a second. That doesn't sound right. Let's just assume they offer the $100,000 before you file suit.

LAWYER: Right.

YOU: Let's say they break it down like this: $25,000 to me, $25,000 to my wife, and $50,000 for our son.

LAWYER: That sounds about right. Very possible.

YOU: So, for me and my wife, you get a third of $10,000 each.

LAWYER: Exactly.

YOU: That's a third of $20,000. So your fee would be $6,666.

LAWYER: Right.

YOU: Now, for our son, in this example, you want to charge 25 percent of the full $50,000. That's $12,500.

LAWYER: Yes. That's likely to be approved by the court.

YOU: But they already offered me $25,000 for his case. Why can't you also do the same for him—a third of anything over

$25,000? If he got $50,000, you'd get a third of $25,000. That's $8,333. Oh, and thirty-three cents.

LAWYER: You didn't let me finish. A guardianship will have to be established. Our firm usually charges a few thousand dollars for that. Plus, an annual accounting has to be filed until he's eighteen. That's ten more years. We generally charge $500 for each accounting. I'm proposing that our firm will handle all of that at no charge to you, other than court filing fees of about $200. So you're still saving a lot of money.

YOU: But don't you usually waive those guardianship fees anyway when you're representing a minor in a personal injury claim?

LAWYER: It depends on the amount of the settlement and the amount of time we've had to put in the case.

YOU: Well, here we're talking about almost no time on your part, especially if there's no lawsuit.

LAWYER: That's true. That's why I'm offering you this deal.

YOU: What if they don't come up with the $100,000 in time and you file suit?

LAWYER: Okay. I would do 40 percent over the first $15,000 for you and your wife. And 30 percent of the full settlement for your son. Again, no additional fees for the guardianship.

YOU: So, we'd still be shooting for the $100,000 after suit.

LAWYER: That's right.

YOU: After suit, let's say we get $25,000 for me, $25,000 for my wife and $50,000 for our son. Then your fee would be 40 percent of $20,000 and 30 percent of $50,000 for our son. That's $23,000 total for fees, compared to about $19,000 without suit.

LAWYER: That sounds very reasonable, considering all the extra work involved in litigation.

YOU: Can my wife and I discuss this privately for a few minutes?

LAWYER: Sure.

So, the lawyer leaves the room. Let's try some multiple choice again. What do you do?

A. Leave the office and look for another lawyer.

B. Take the deal.

C. Take the deal for you and your wife, but insist on the same terms for your son.

D. Make a counteroffer for all three of your claims.

Well, if you chose B, you've got to return to "Go" and read the whole book over again. Remember, it can't hurt to try for something better, unless you're in a take it or leave it situation. Obviously, this is not one of those situations. What about looking for another lawyer? You're in this lawyer's office because you liked the way he treated you from the start. He gave you the right advice on trying to settle on your own. He indicated a willingness to work with you if you hired him. At this point, he's just showing you some of his own negotiating ability. He's trying to get the best deal he can under the circumstances, just like you. Don't give up on him for that. Admire him. But don't give in to him, either.

So, the choices are C or D. Why should you agree to the lawyer's proposal for you and your wife? You've got nothing to lose by trying for a better deal for all of you. If you chose D, you're really thinking like a true negotiator.

What kind of counteroffer do you make? Incidentally, that was a good move when you asked to be alone with your wife. You took the momentum away from the lawyer. You took the pressure off. You gave yourselves the time and space to come up with your next move. What will it be?

A. Ten percent of anything over $55,000 without a lawsuit; 20 percent of anything over $55,000 with suit.

B. A flat fee of $3,000 if settled without suit, only if the full $100,000 is received; 20 percent of anything over $55,000 with suit.

C. Thirty percent over $55,000 without suit; 35 percent over $55,000 with suit.

D. Twenty-five percent over $30,000 without suit for you and your wife; 15 percent of total settlement for your son without suit. With suit, 30 percent over $30,000 for you and your wife; 20 percent of total settlement for your son.

Which of the four choices did you eliminate first? If you knocked out C, you're doing well. This choice is just too close to the attorney's offer. He said he would take 33 1/3 percent for you and your wife without suit. If you counteroffer with 30 percent, you're just not giving yourself enough room to negotiate. Let's say the lawyer gets you and your wife a total of $50,000, $20,000 more than you were offered on your own. The fee difference is 3 1/3 percent of $20,000, or a little over $600. You're trying to save yourself more than that.

How about the flat fee proposition in choice B? At first glance, it doesn't sound too bad. In effect, you're offering the lawyer less than 7 percent of $45,000 for doing very little work—that is, getting the $100,000 without suit. But you're also putting a restriction on your own flexibility to decide to settle without suit for less than $100,000. Let's assume that the adjuster offers $95,000 before the 30 days period expires. If you agree to deal B, you don't even have the option of accepting the $95,000. You've backed yourself into a corner, forcing a suit that you may not want or need. Always allow yourself as many options as possible.

What about choice D? You're giving yourself some room to negotiate. You're going along with the framework proposal by your lawyer, separating the fee structure on your son's case. But why do this? The lawyer only said that your son's settlement must be court approved. He didn't say that the court required that the fee agreement be structured in a certain way. We know that your son's case has the greatest settlement value. Why give the lawyer the opportunity to make so much more? For example, let's say you settle without suit for the full $100,000, but the adjuster breaks it down as follows: $15,000 for you, $15,000 for your wife, $70,000 for your son. In choice D, the lawyer takes no fee on your wife's settlement or yours, however, he gets 15 percent of $70,000, or $10,500 for your son's case. In choice A, he gets a fee of only 10 percent over $45,000, which is $4,500. That's

$6,000 more in his pocket if you agreed to deal D. And he hardly had to do any work to get it.

Let's assume you have productive negotiations with your lawyer. You counteroffer with choice A. You finally agree on a reasonable compromise: 20 percent over $55,000 without suit; 30 percent over $55,000 with suit. The $55,000 is itemized based on the adjuster's breakdown. The firm will also handle the guardianship and waive all attorney's fees.

Your lawyer faxes the adjuster a letter the next day, standing firm on the $100,000 and the time limit. Three days later, the adjuster offers $80,000: $20,000 to you, $20,000 to your wife, and $40,000 to your son. You all agree not to accept.

The adjuster makes no further offers within the time limit. On the thirty-first day, your lawyer files suit. He sends a copy to the adjuster. Four days later, the adjuster offers the full $100,000. He breaks it down $25,000 to you, $25,000 to your wife, and $50,000 to your son.

You discuss the possibility of bad faith with your lawyer. He explains it would require two trials. In the first trial, a jury would have to award a total of more than the $100,000 for your three claims. In the second trial, another jury would have to decide that your insurance company demonstrated bad faith when they could have settled the case without suit for $100,000. The lawyer says these trials could take years, and involve many thousands of dollars in court costs. There is no guarantee you will be successful in both trials. Even if you are, it may not be worth fighting for, especially if the judgment was not much more than $100,000.

You decide to accept the $100,000. You and your wife receive your settlement quickly. The lawyer takes his fee of 30 percent of $20,000, plus $200 for costs of filing the suit. So, out of the $50,000 allocated to you and your wife, you walk away with $43,800.

Finalizing your son's case will take some time. Your lawyer files papers to set up the guardianship. A hearing is scheduled for the probate judge to approve the settlement. You and your wife will be present. But your best bet is to let the judge and lawyer do the talking. It might go something like this:

JUDGE: This is a $50,000 gross settlement?

LAWYER: Yes, your honor.

JUDGE: Wasn't it a $100,000 policy?

LAWYER: Yes, your honor. But the insurance company allocated it $50,000 to the minor, and $25,000 to each of the parents. Both parents had herniated discs.

JUDGE: Did you make separate demands?

LAWYER: No, your honor. It was a single limit policy. My clients initially demanded the policy limits prior to hiring me. When I was retained, I reiterated the policy limit demand on behalf of my three clients. The limits were only tendered after I filed suit.

JUDGE: I'm looking at the proposed settlement statement. You show your fee as $7,500. How did you arrive at that?

LAWYER: Prior to my representation, the carrier offered my clients $25,000 for settlement of the minor's claim. When they hired me, we negotiated an agreement whereby once the suit was filed I would receive 30 percent of any amount recovered over the $25,000. This was the same arrangement I had for the parent's claims.

JUDGE: Did you have a lower percentage without suit?

LAWYER: Yes, your honor.

JUDGE: What was it?

LAWYER: Twenty percent of the recovery over $25,000.

JUDGE: How long after you filed suit did you settle?

LAWYER: I don't recall exactly—within about a week.

JUDGE: So defense counsel had not yet been retained?

LAWYER: That's correct.

JUDGE: Do you feel it's fair to charge this minor the extra 10 percent just for filing suit?

LAWYER: That was our agreement, your honor. I couldn't foresee how far into litigation we'd have to go.

JUDGE: Well, I don't think it's fair. I'm going to ask you to voluntarily reduce your fee back to the 20 percent of recovery over $25,000. So that would be a fee of $5,000 instead of $7,500. If you'd rather not do that, I'll appoint a guardian *ad litem*. But I'm sure that he'd look carefully at your total number of hours in this case, counselor. So, what will it be?

LAWYER: Your honor, I neglected to mention that my firm has agreed to handle the guardianship and all annual accountings at no extra charge.

JUDGE: That's very good of you. But a $5,000 fee should still be more than enough to cover that. So, are we in agreement?

LAWYER: Yes, your honor.

JUDGE: Fine. Counsel has agreed to reduce his fee to $5,000. The $50,000 settlement is approved. You'll prepare the order?

LAWYER: Yes, your honor.

JUDGE: Fine. Good luck to you all.

You certainly were lucky to have this kind of judge. Did you notice how he got your lawyer to "voluntarily agree" to the reduction? The mere mention of appointing a guardian *ad litem* was enough to persuade the lawyer. The judge could have just ordered the reduction without the lawyer's consent. But this judge allowed the lawyer to choose, knowing what his choice would be. Talk about good negotiating.

Hopefully, you have gotten a feel for what's involved in settling a minor's claim. Remember, just because you may need a lawyer doesn't mean you have no leverage. Personal injury lawyers are used to negotiating every day. The more you do it, the more comfortable you'll feel. If you find a lawyer who's not negotiable, look for another one who is.

Index